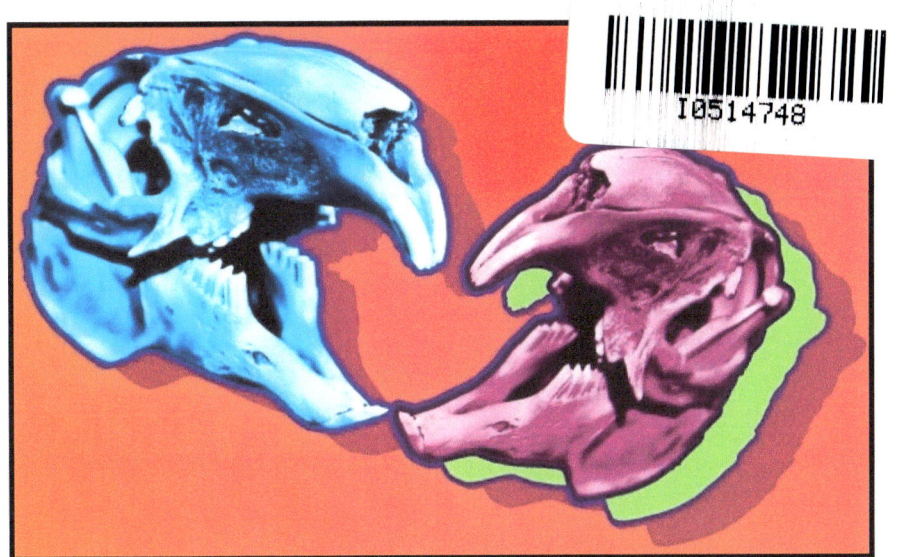

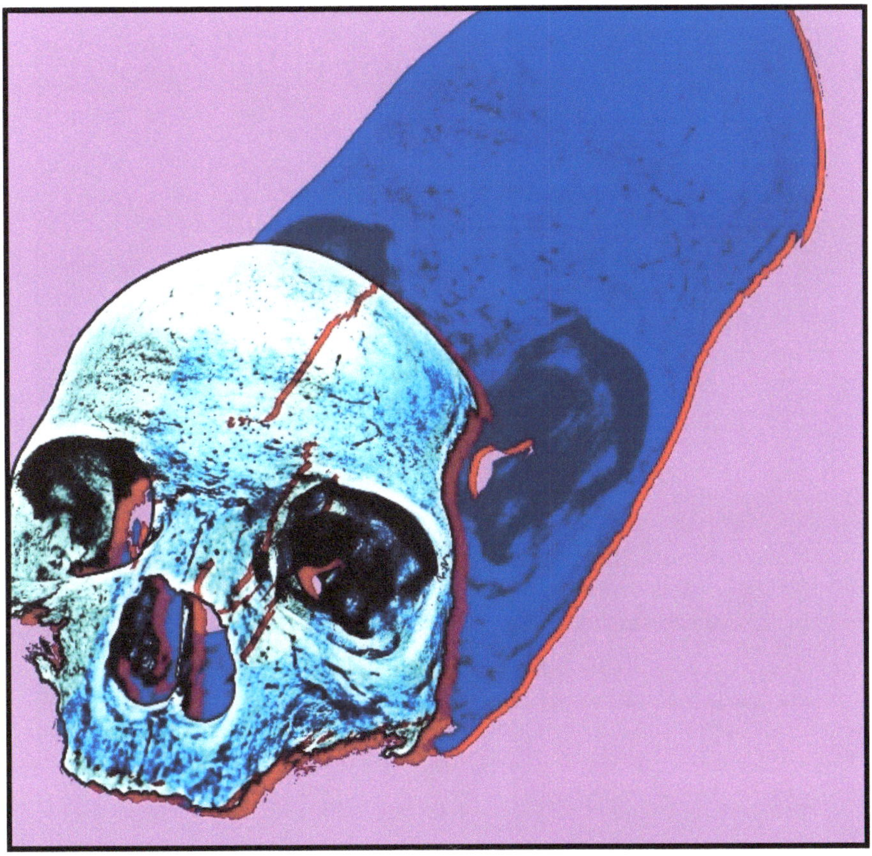

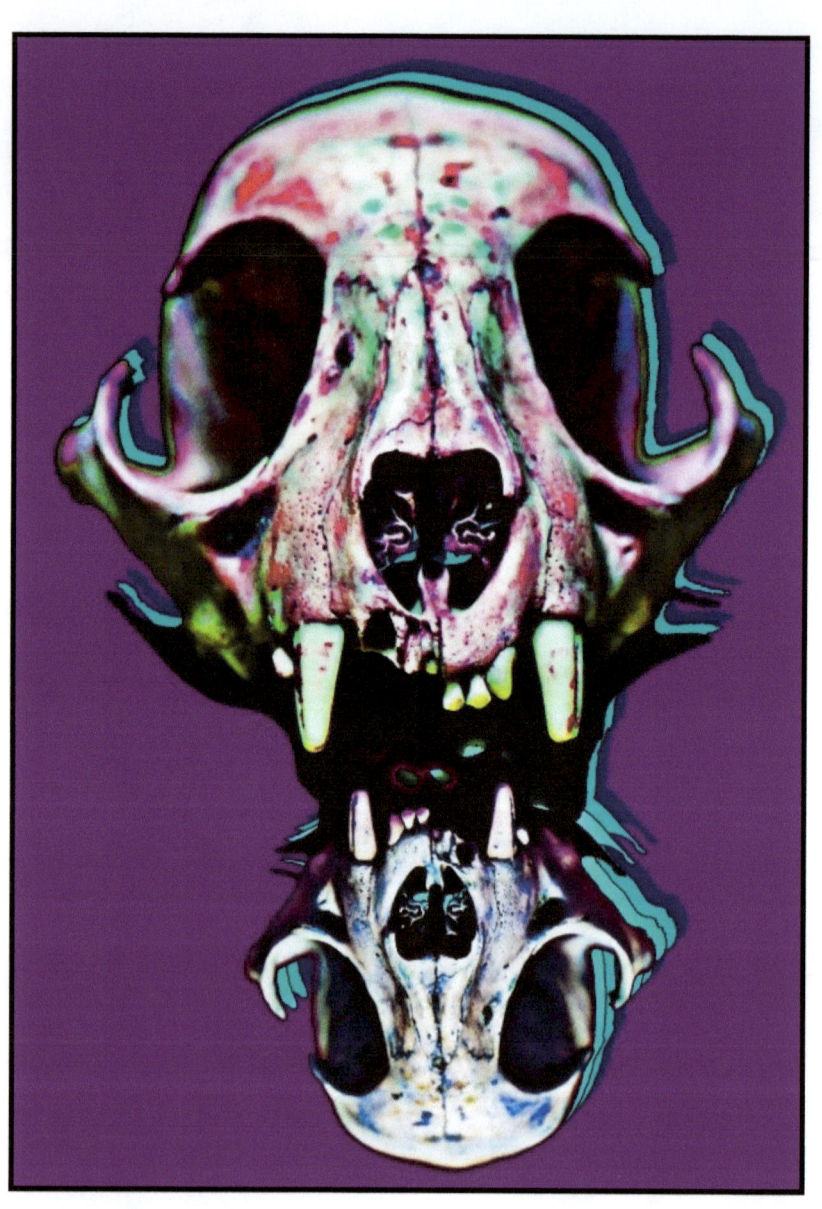

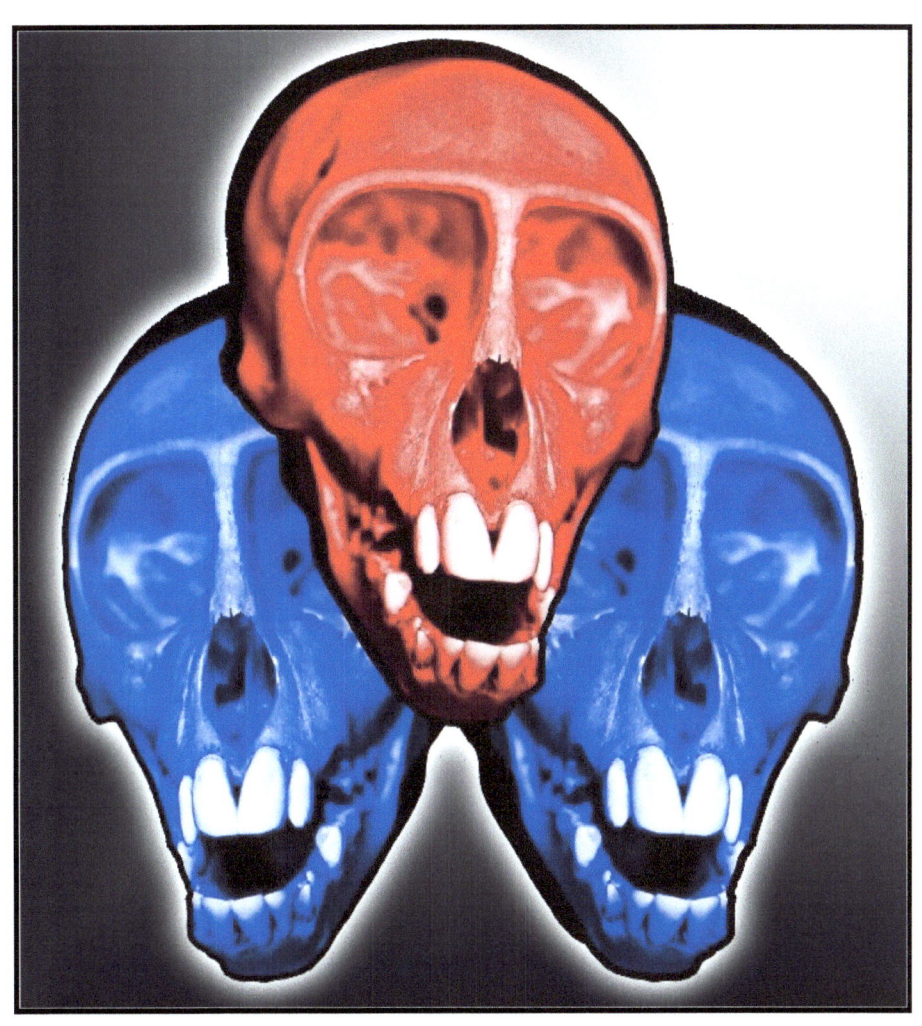

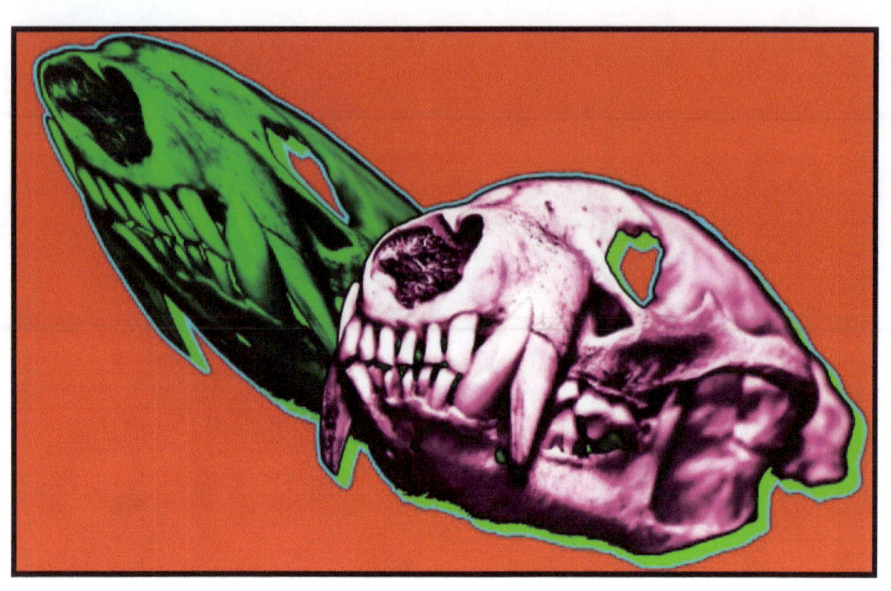

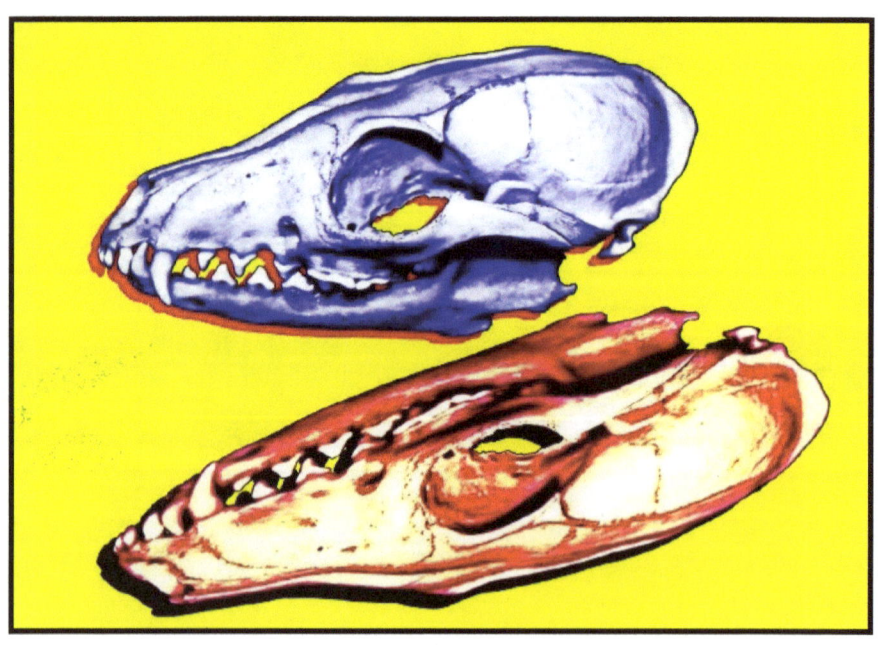

DIAGNOSIS: DOOMED

VOLUME 1

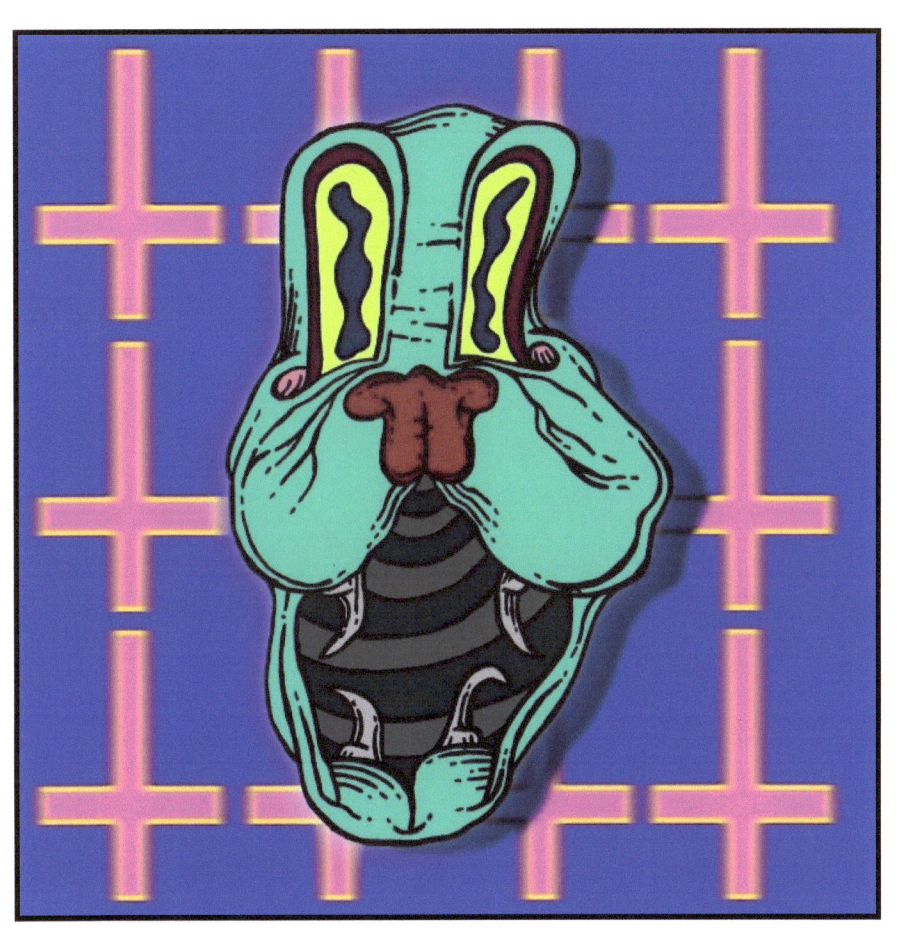

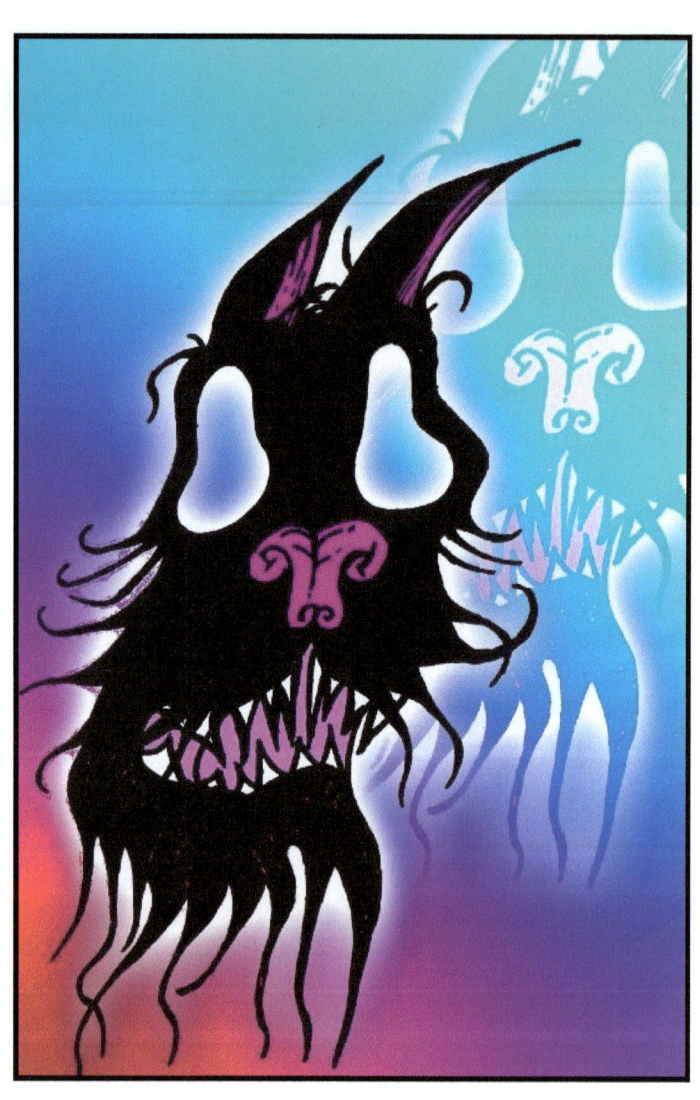

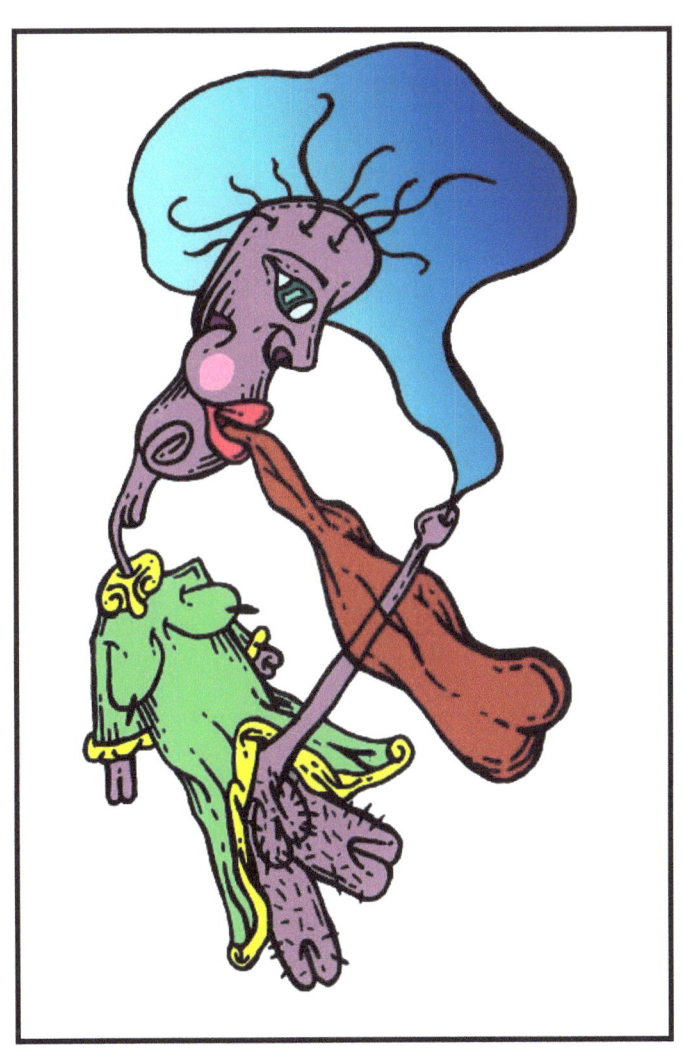

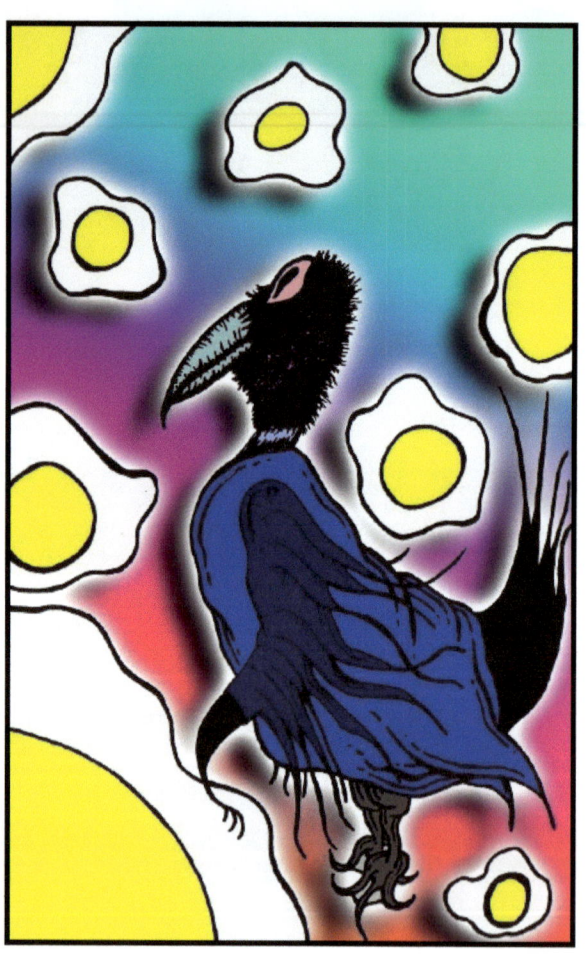

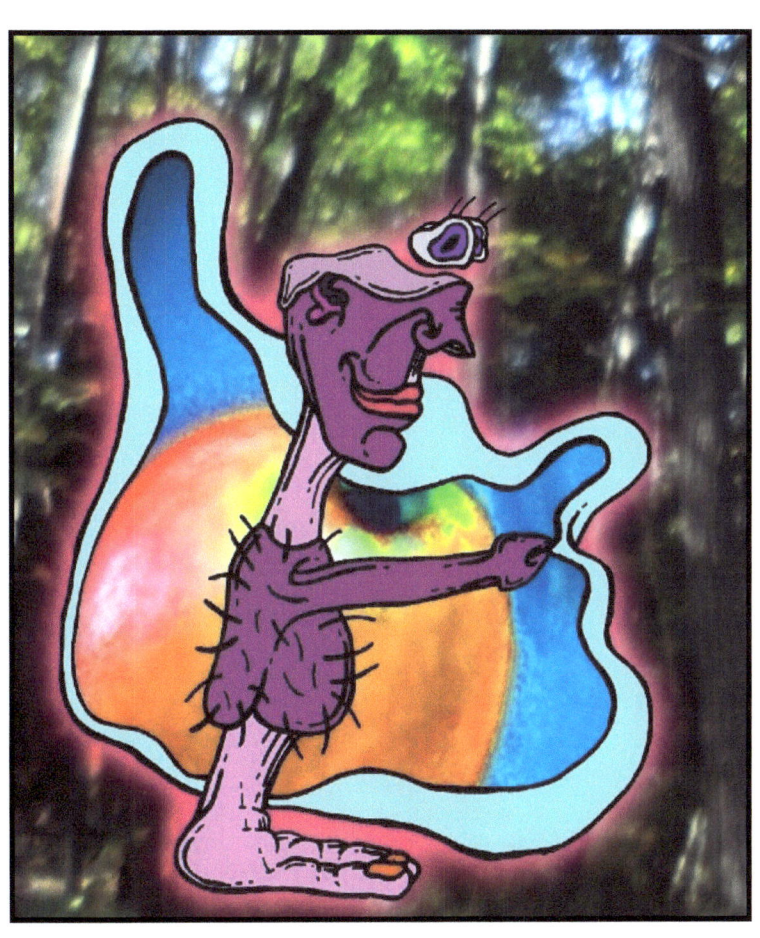

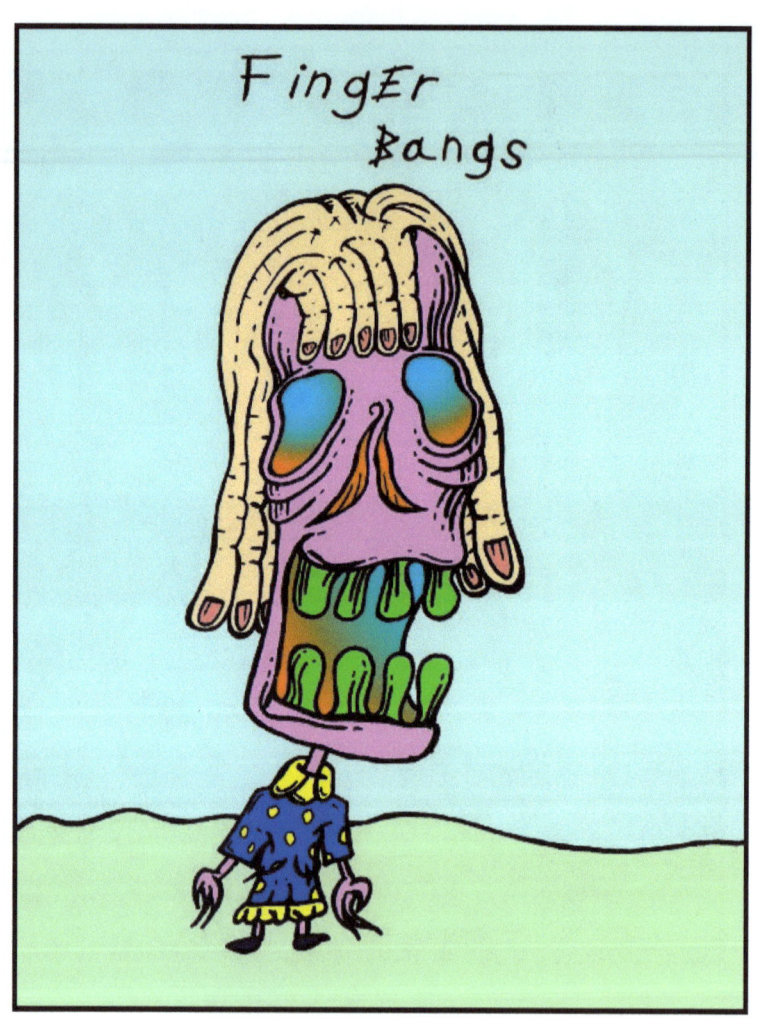

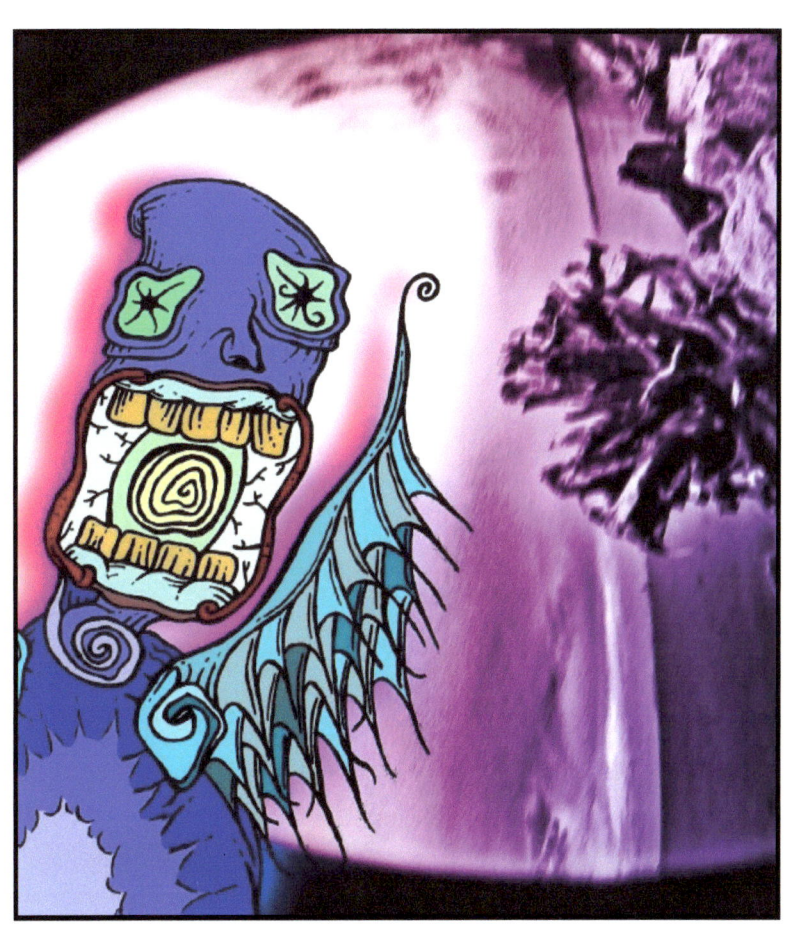

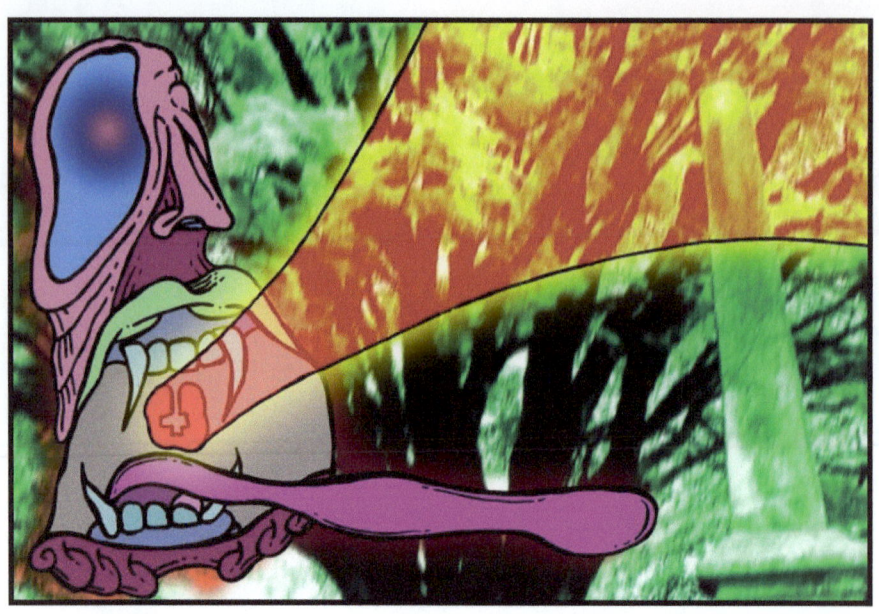

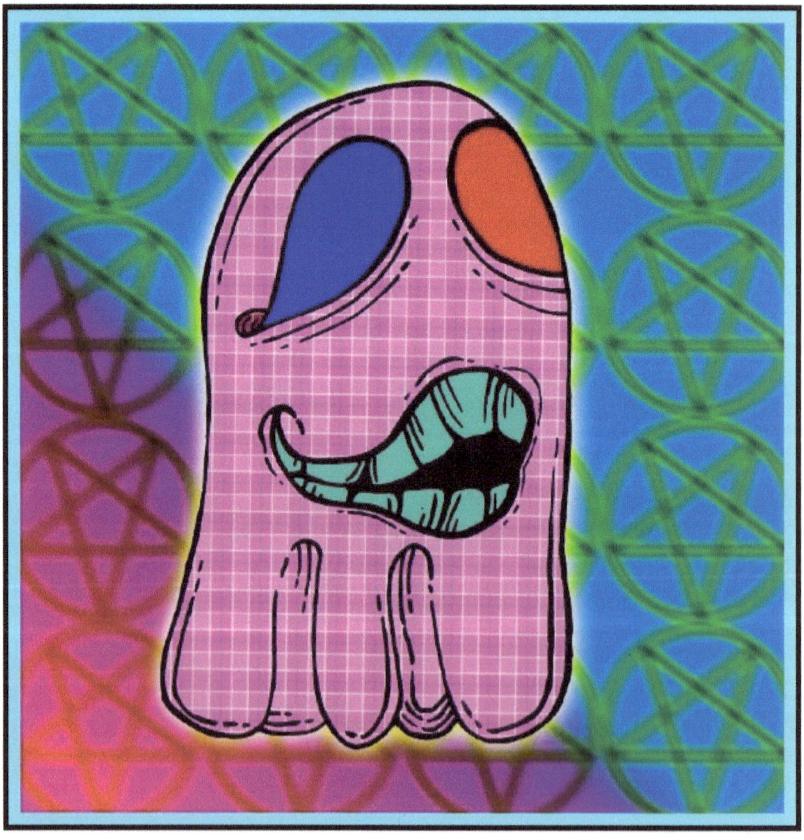

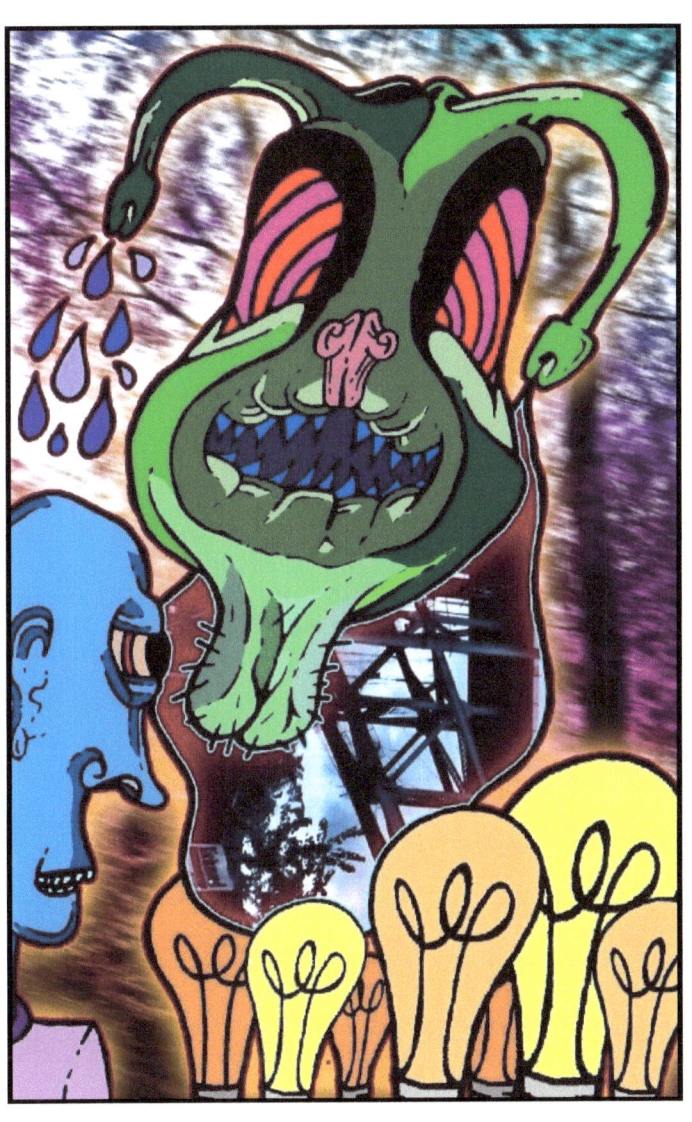

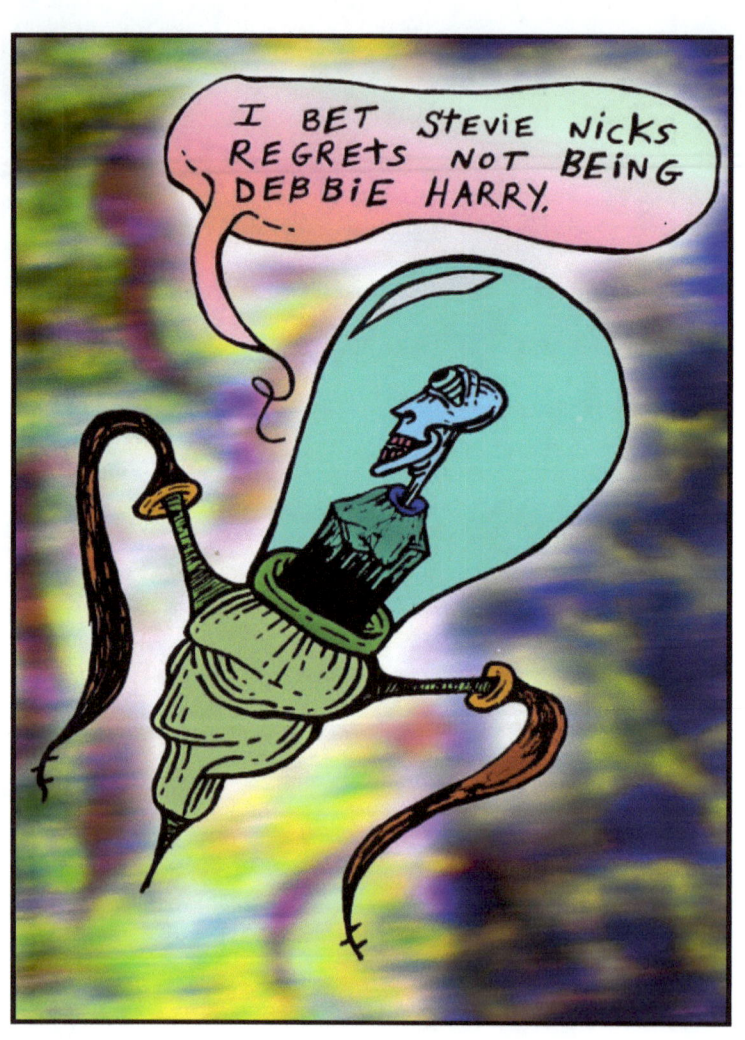

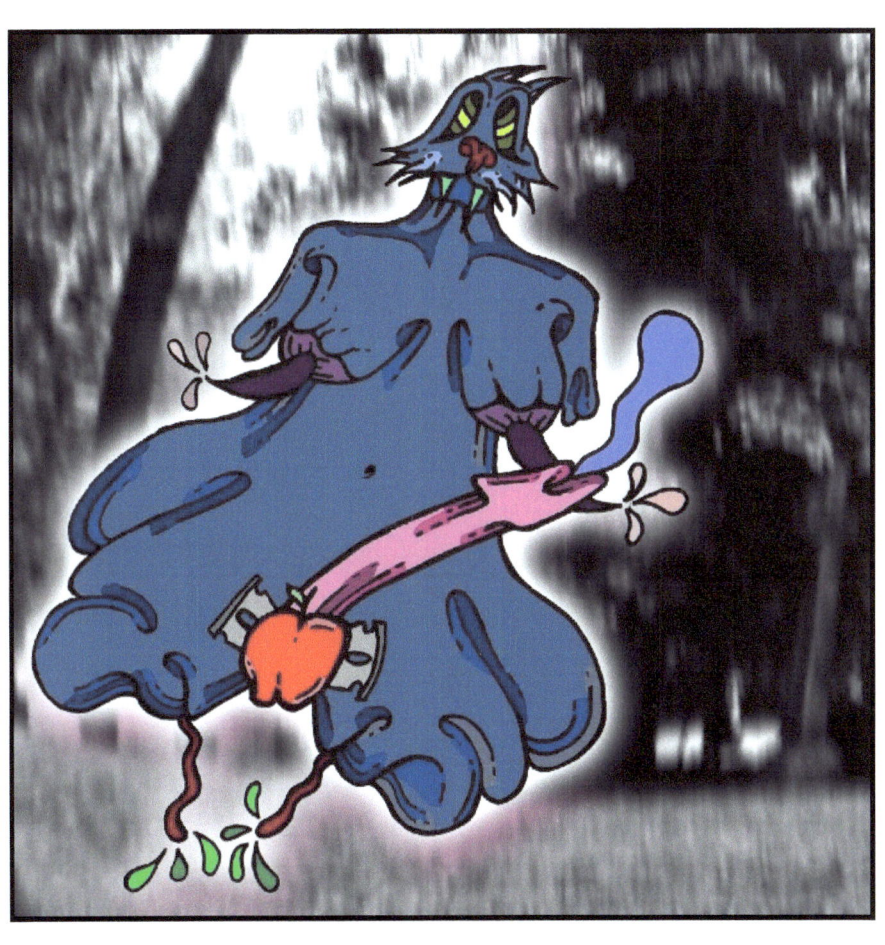

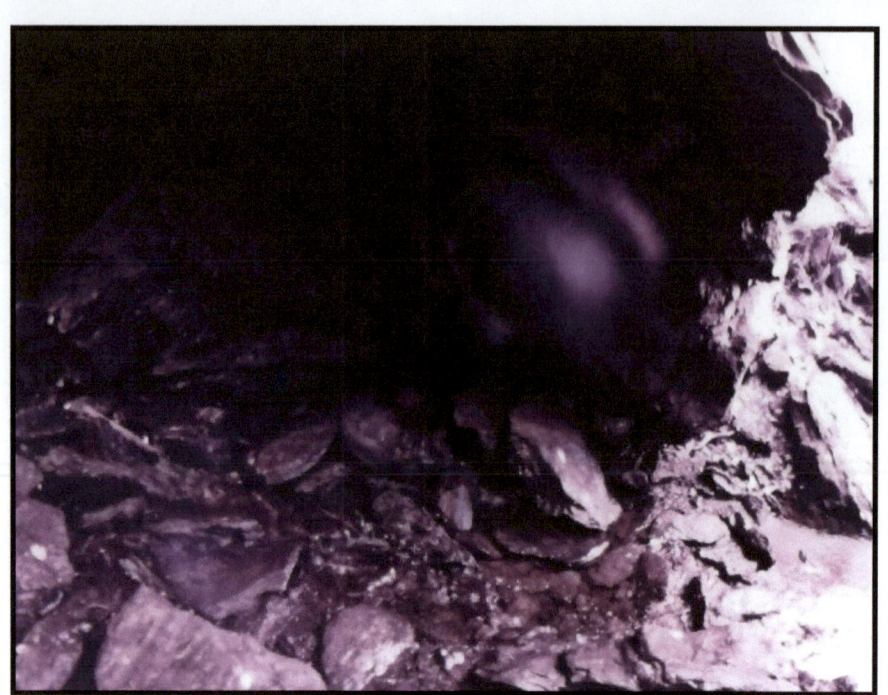

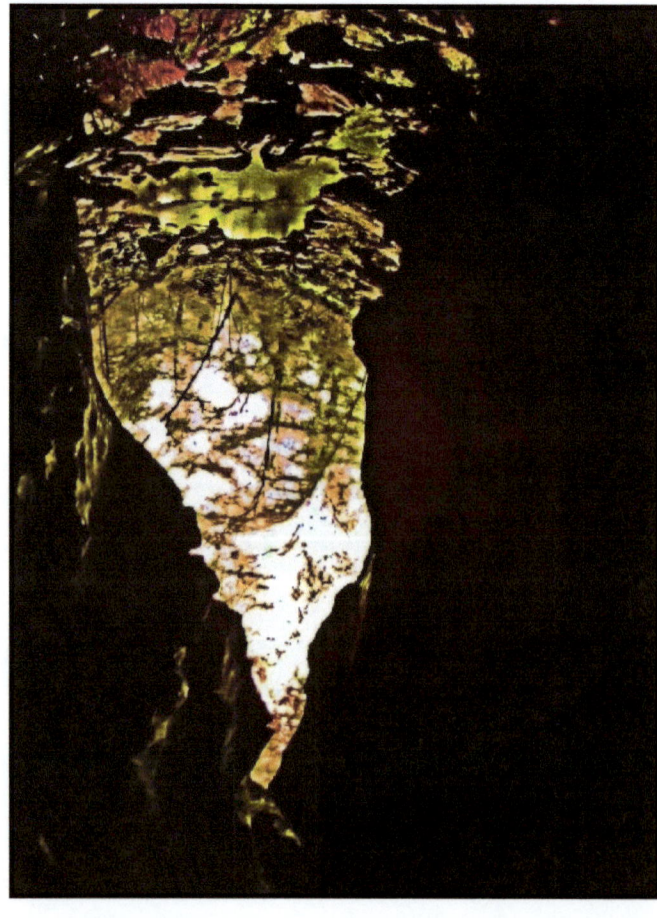

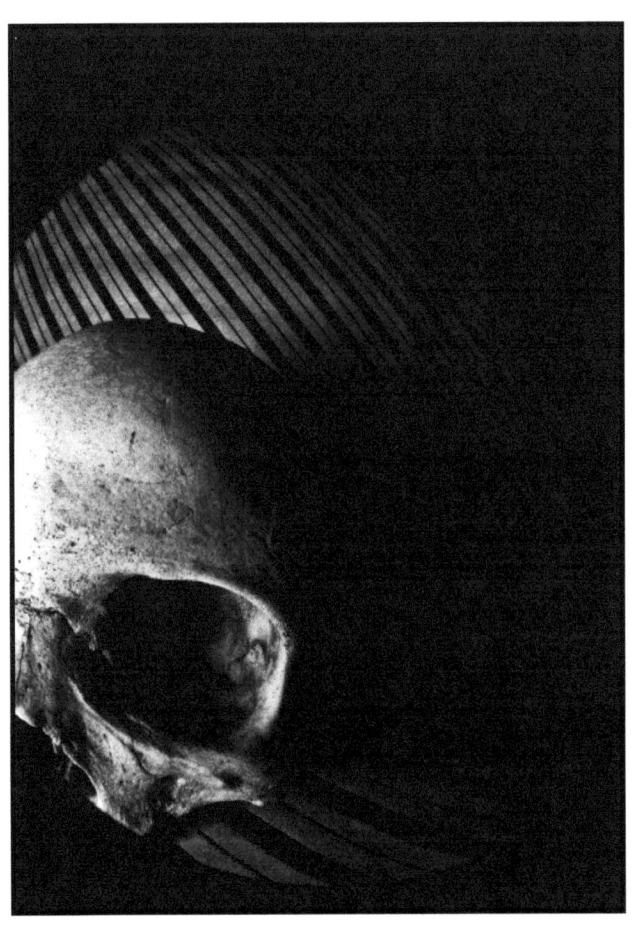

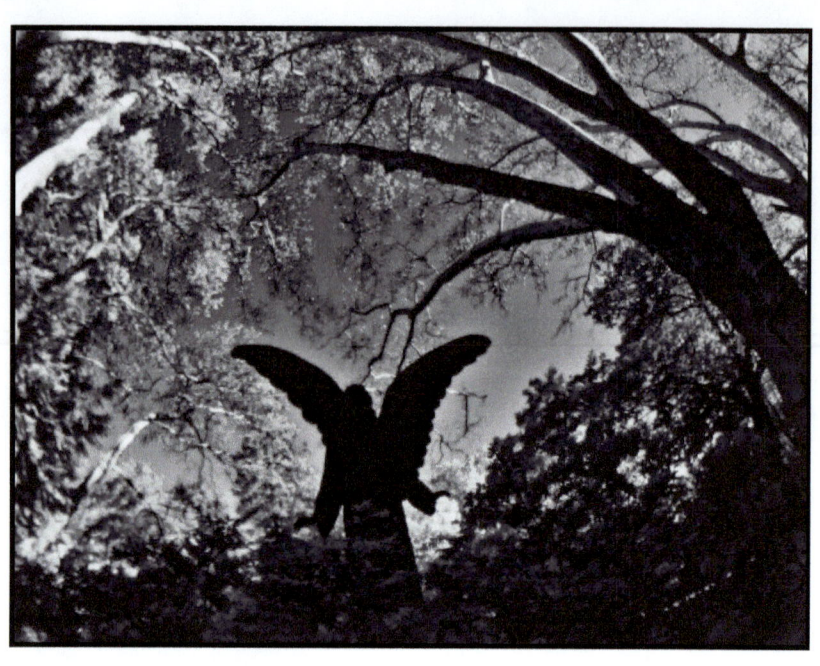

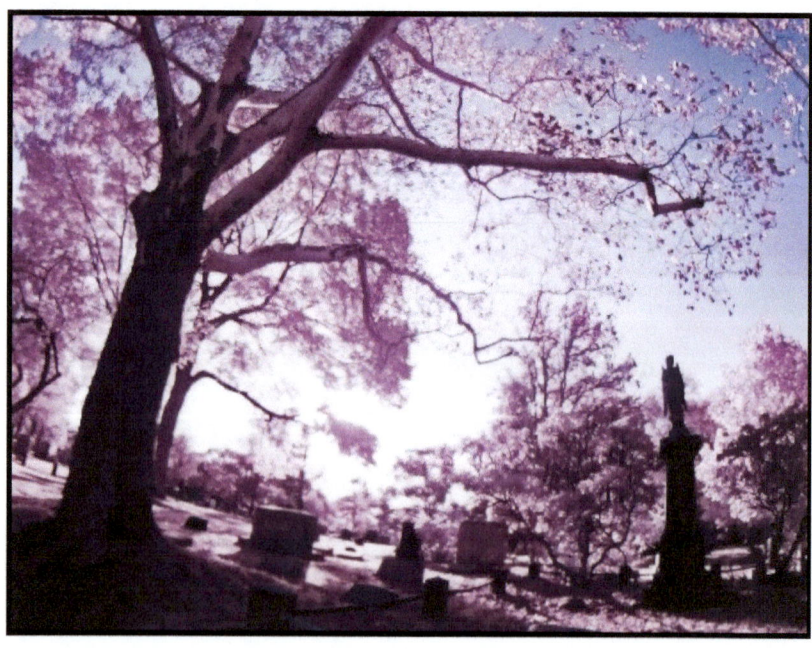

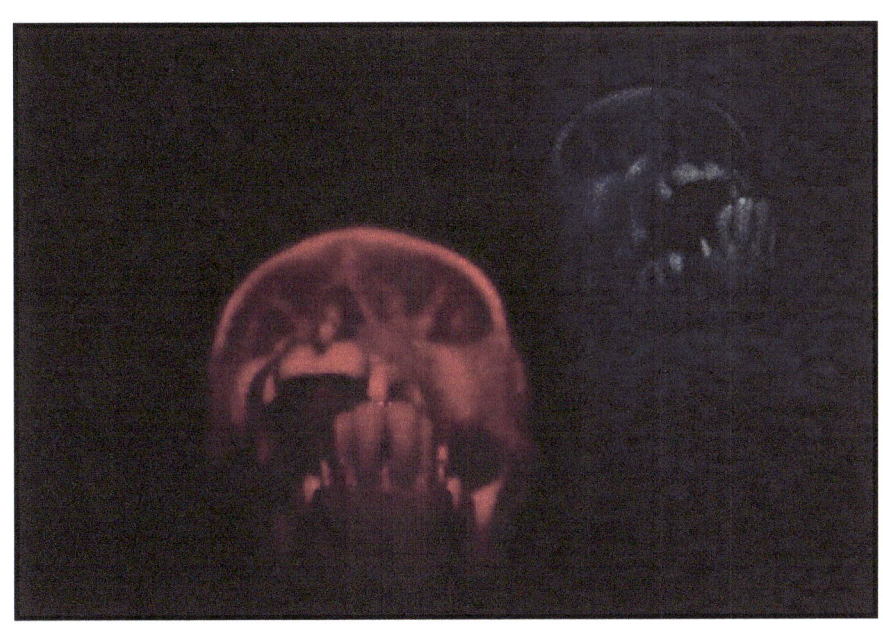

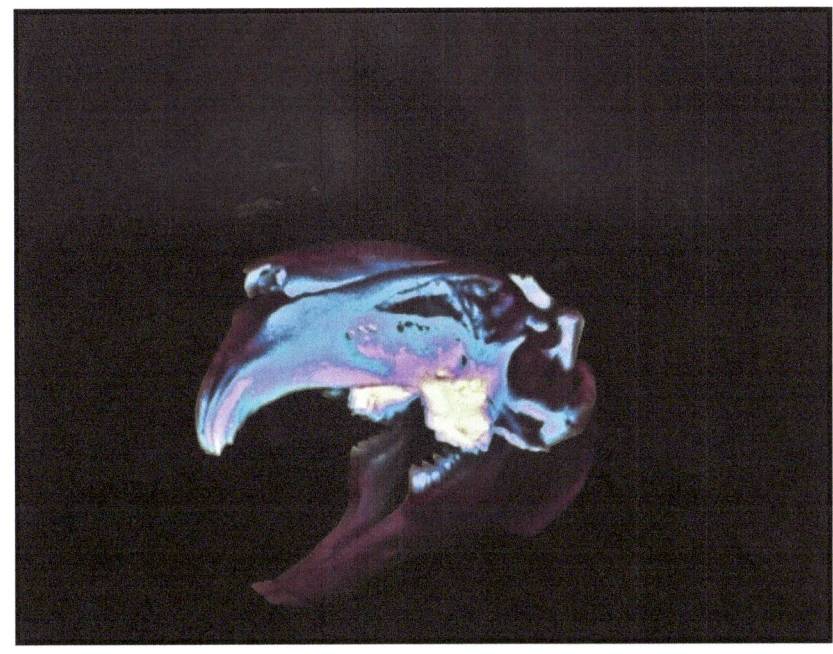

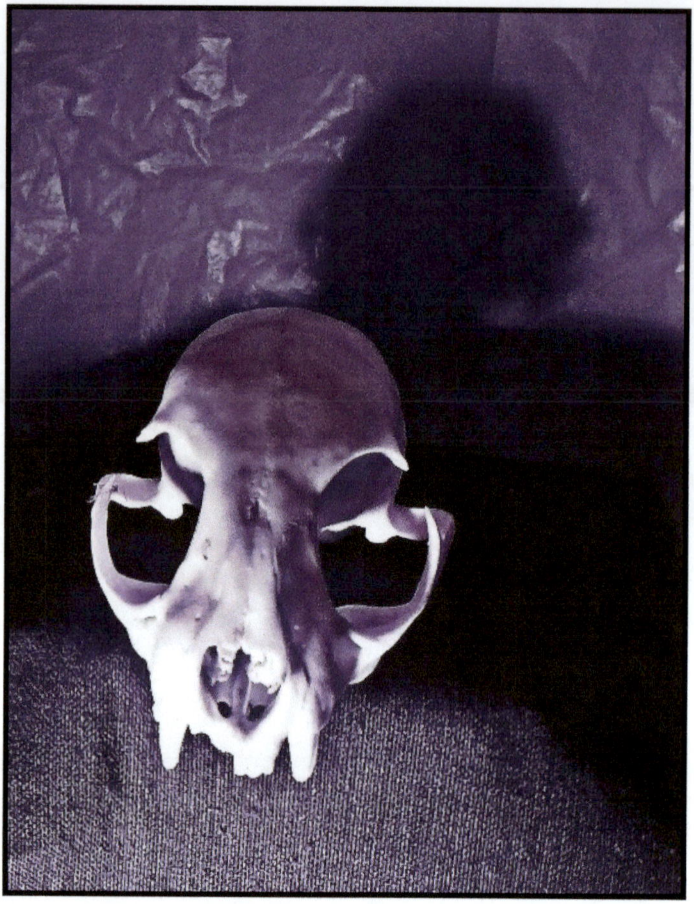

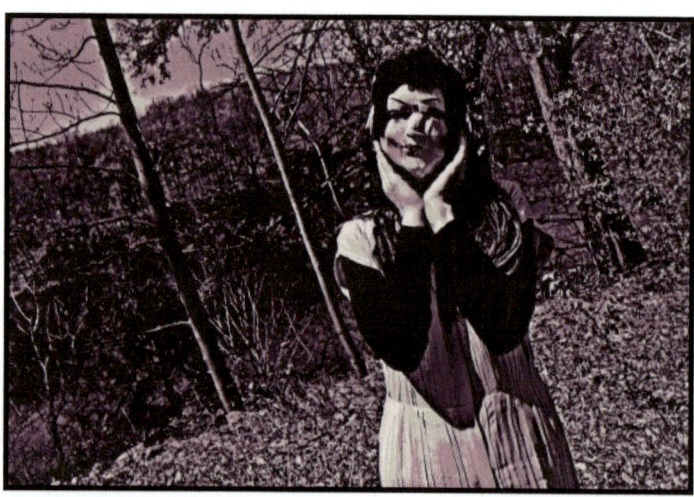

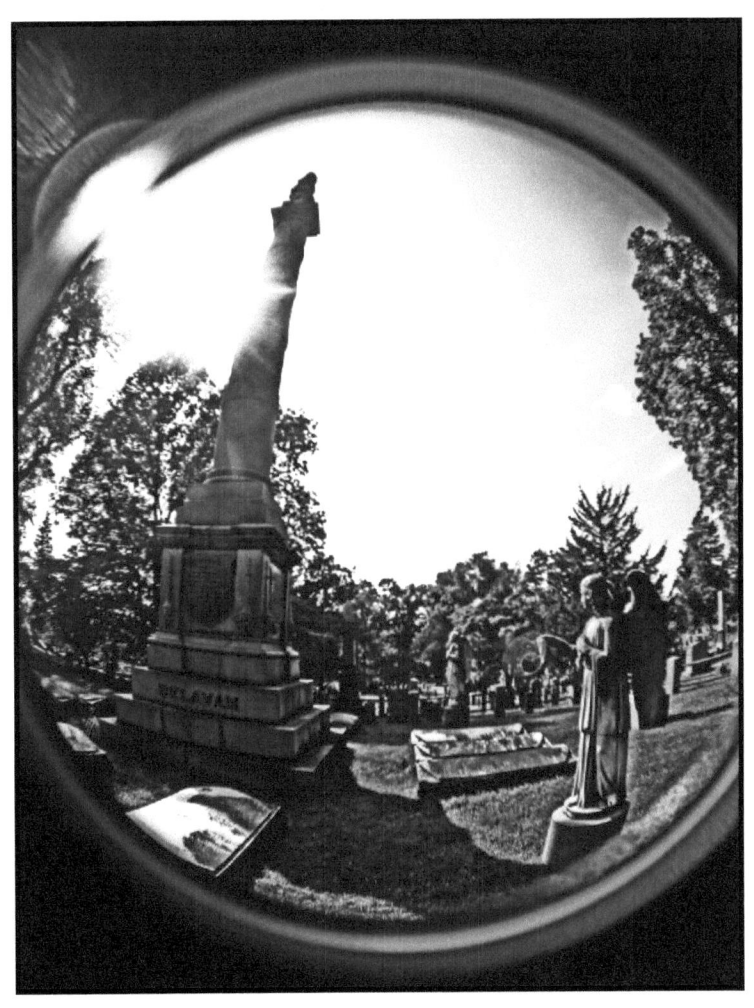

FROM THIS POINT FORWARD IT IS SEPTEMBER OF 2013 AND YOU ARE IN CENTRALIA, PENNSYLVANIA, AND LIKE YOU, I KNOW NONE OF THE PEOPLE IN THESE PHOTOS, EVEN THOUGH I TOOK THEM (THE PHOTOS, NOT THE PEOPLE).

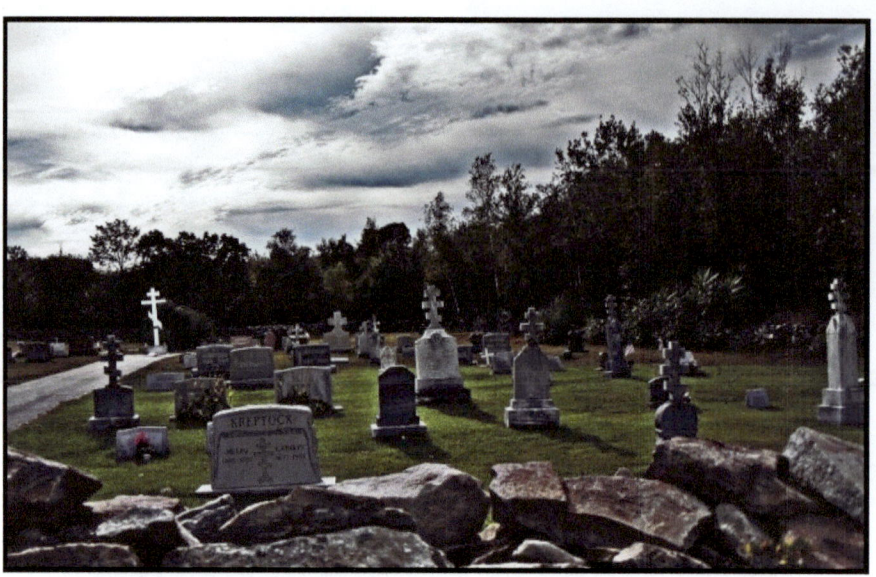

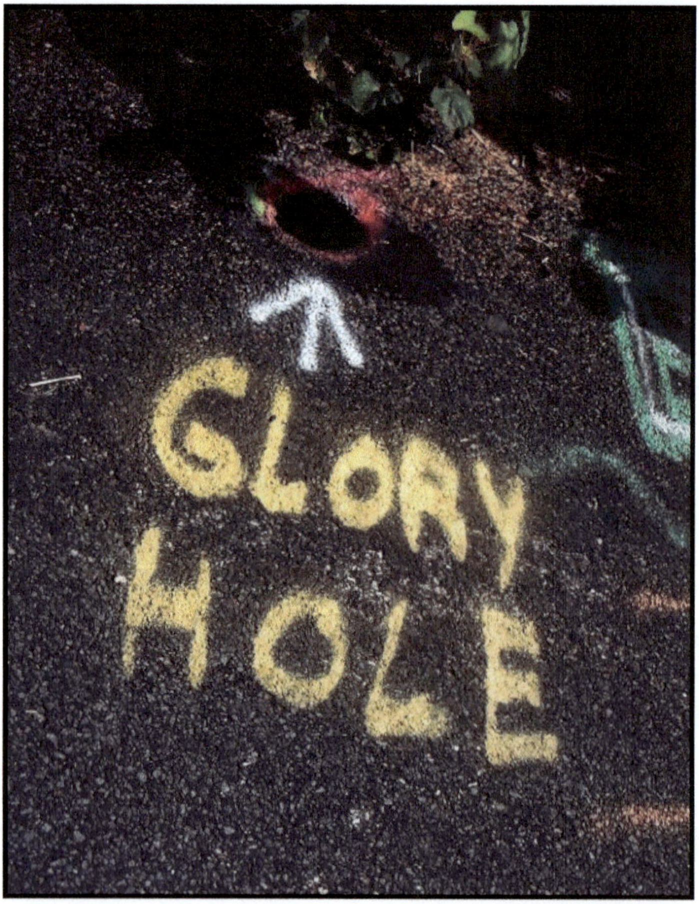

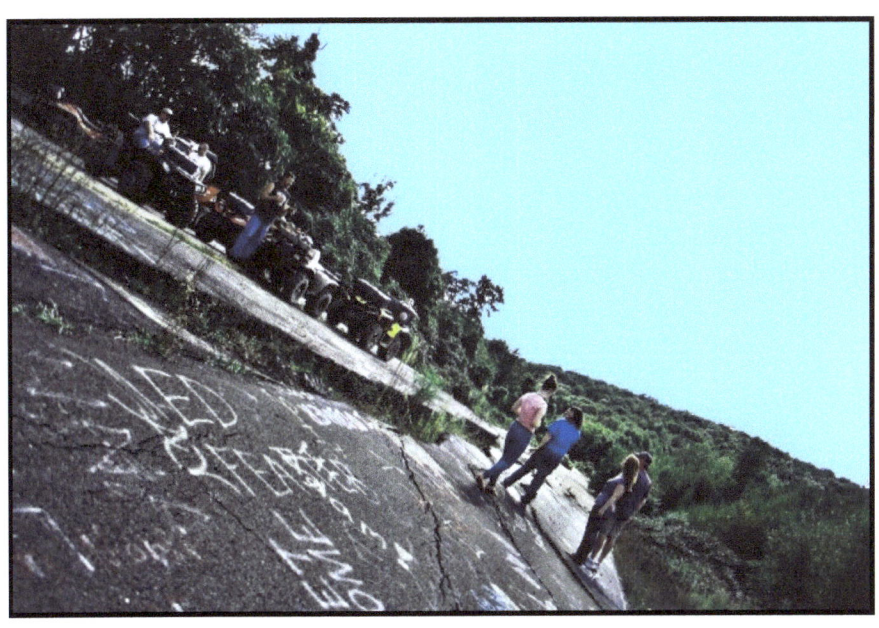

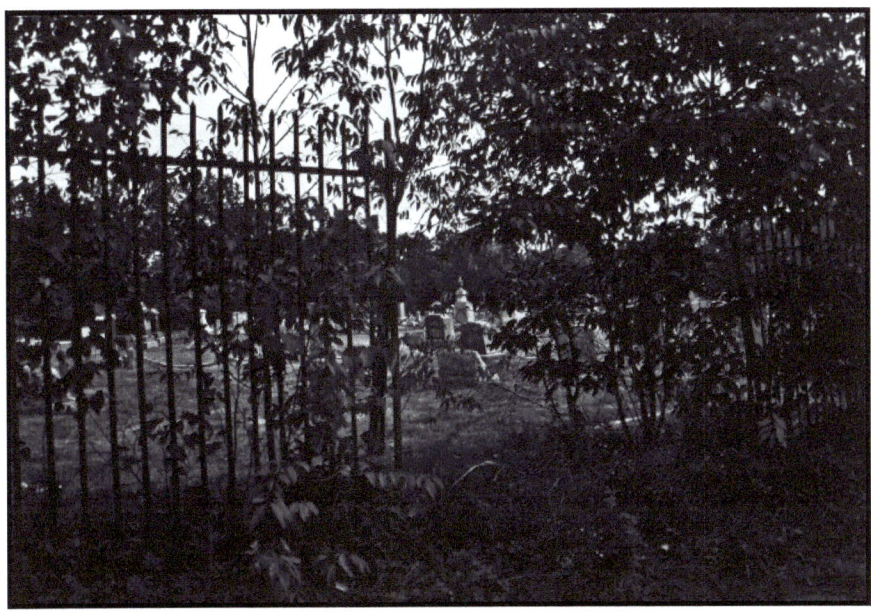

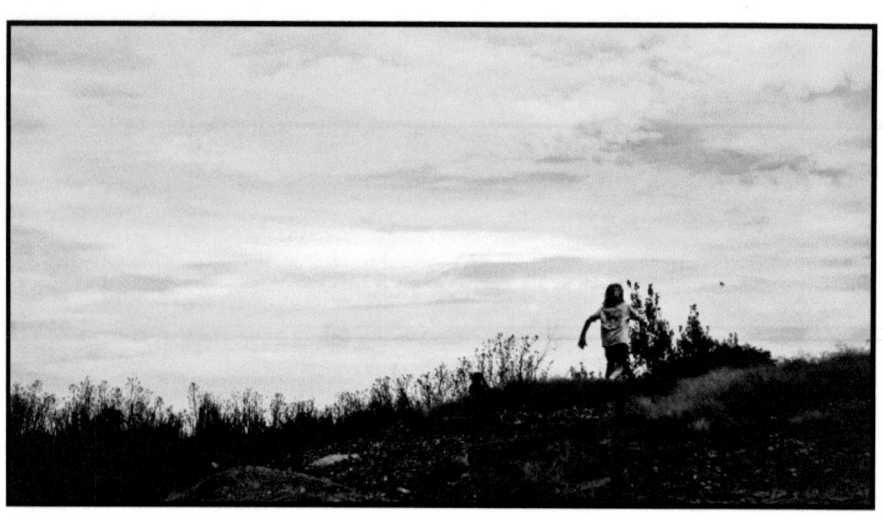

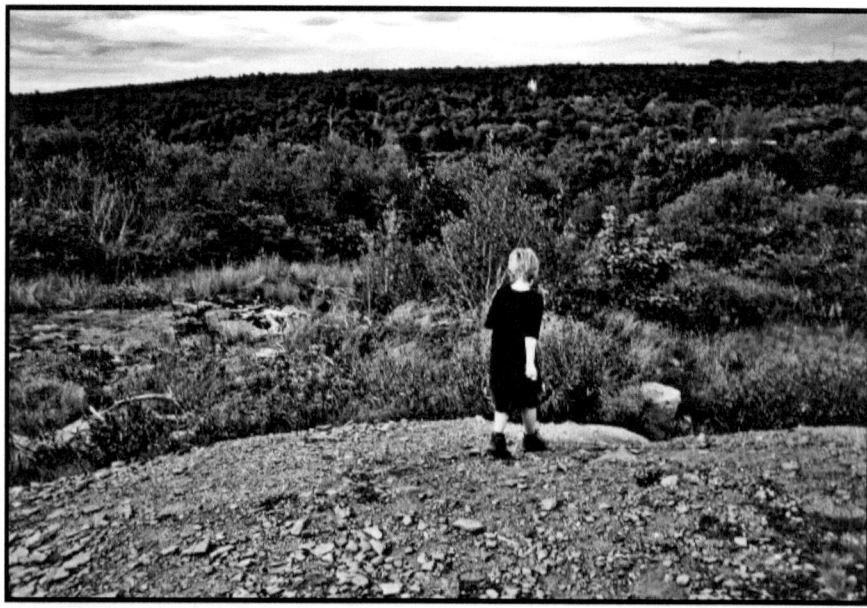

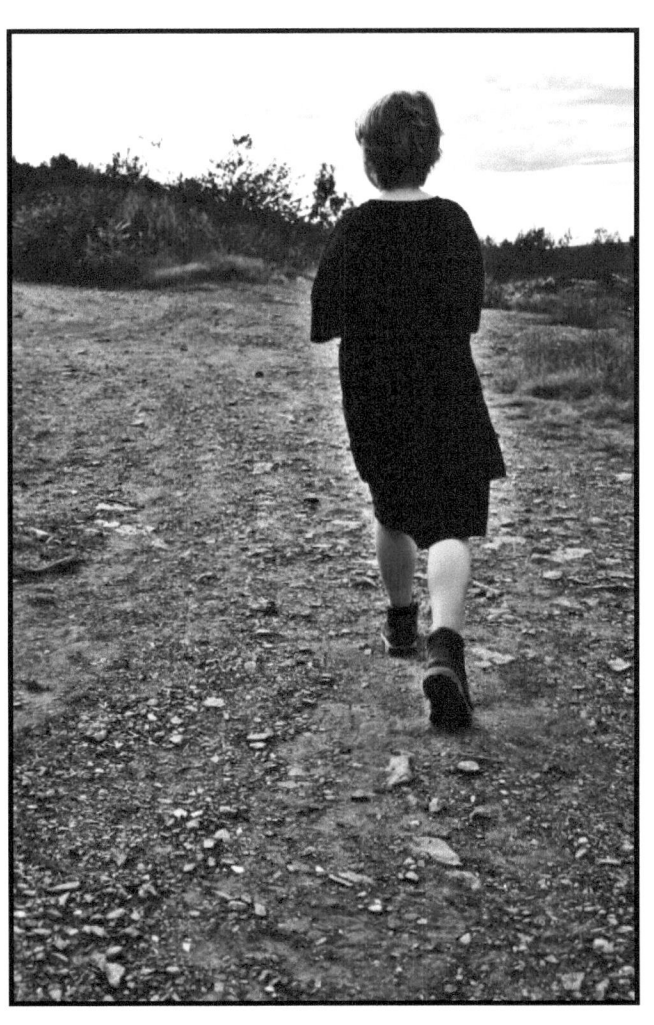

BUT, NOT ANY MORE.

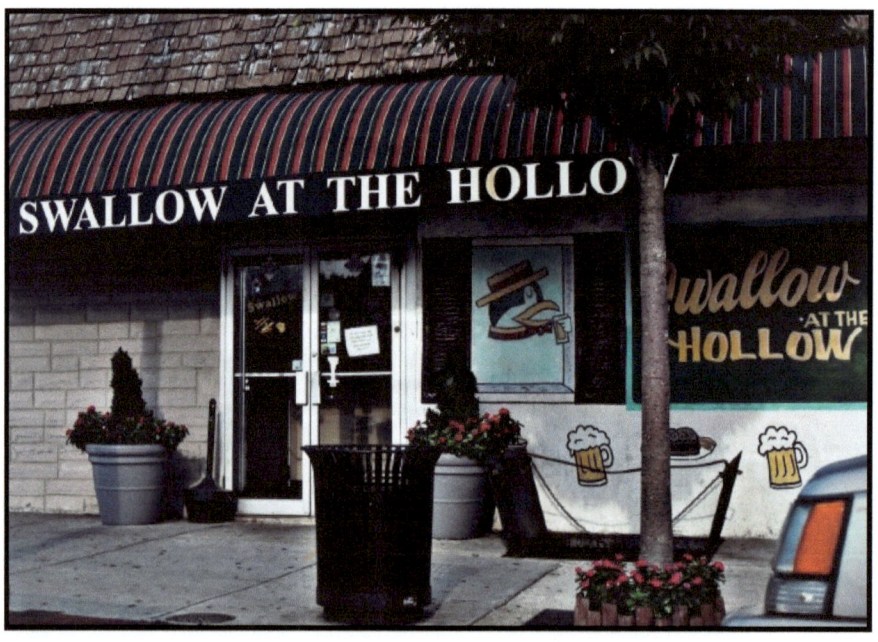

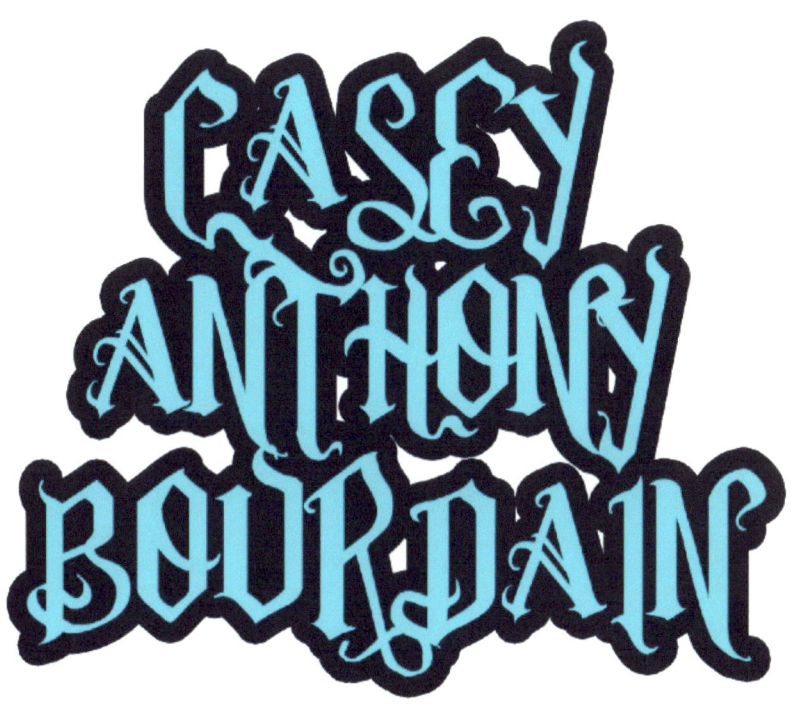

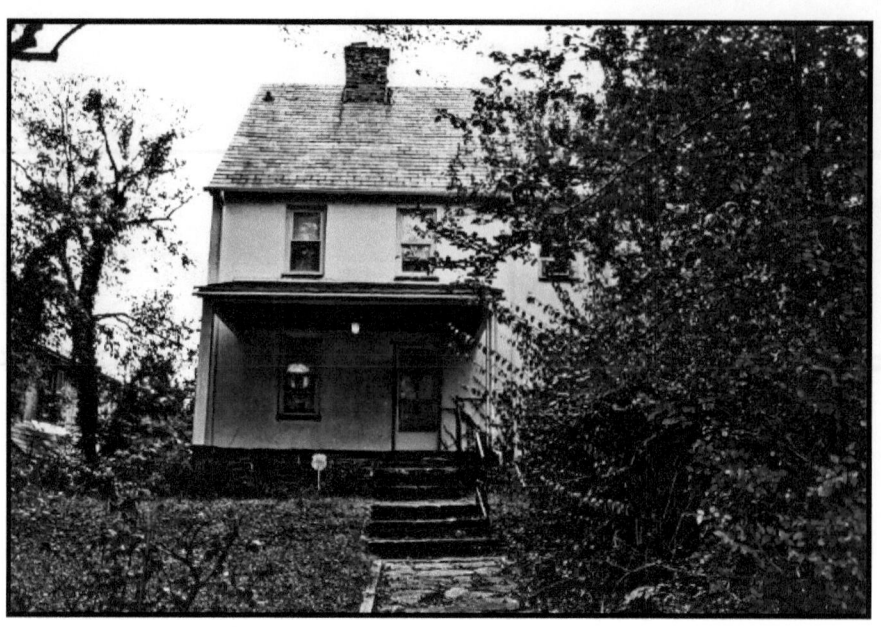

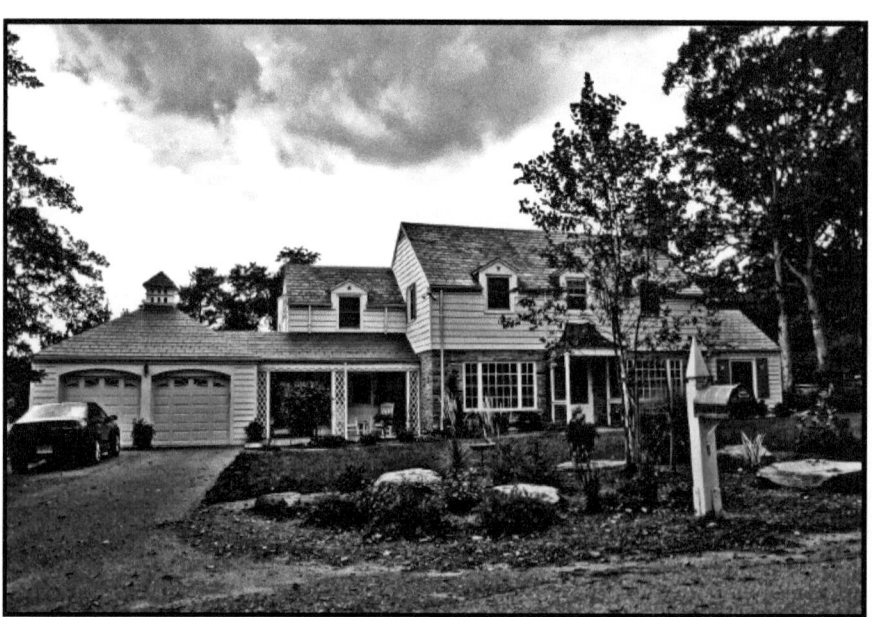

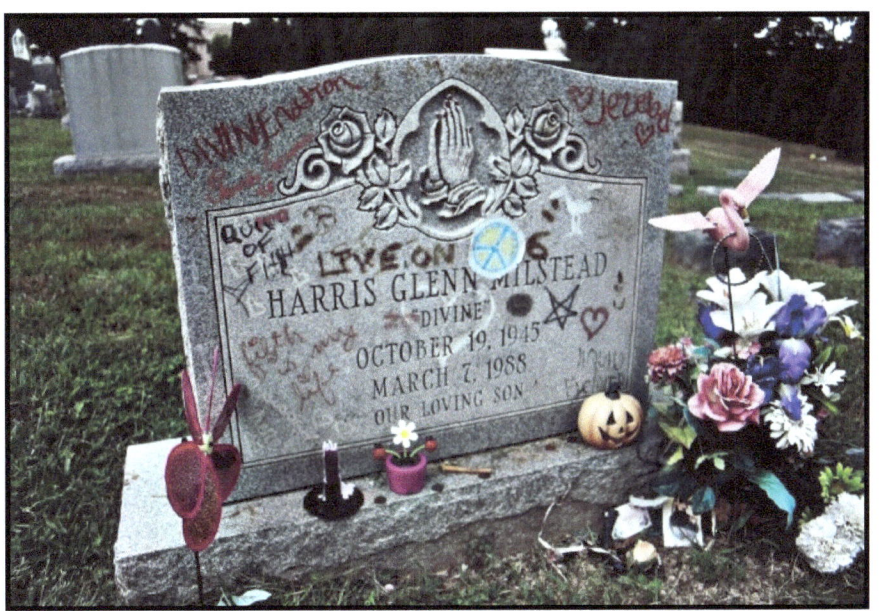

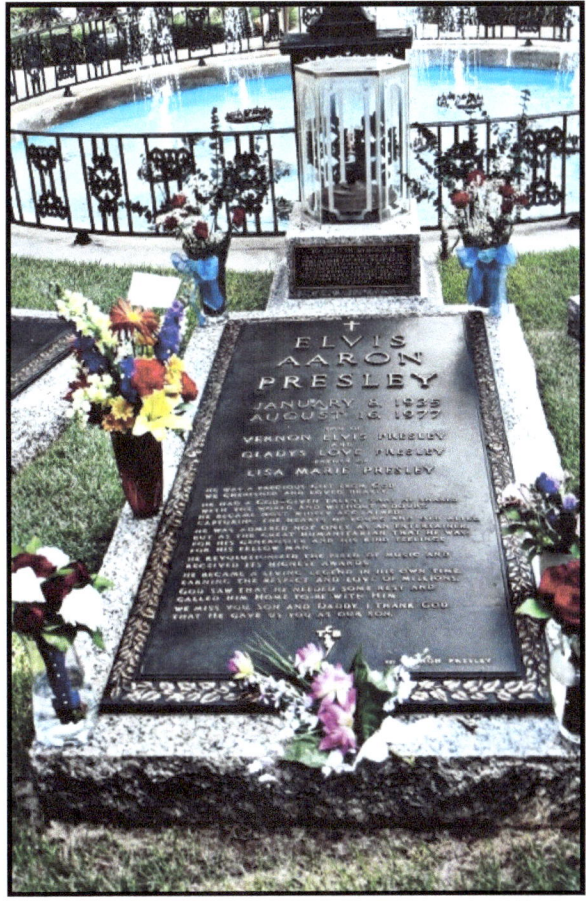

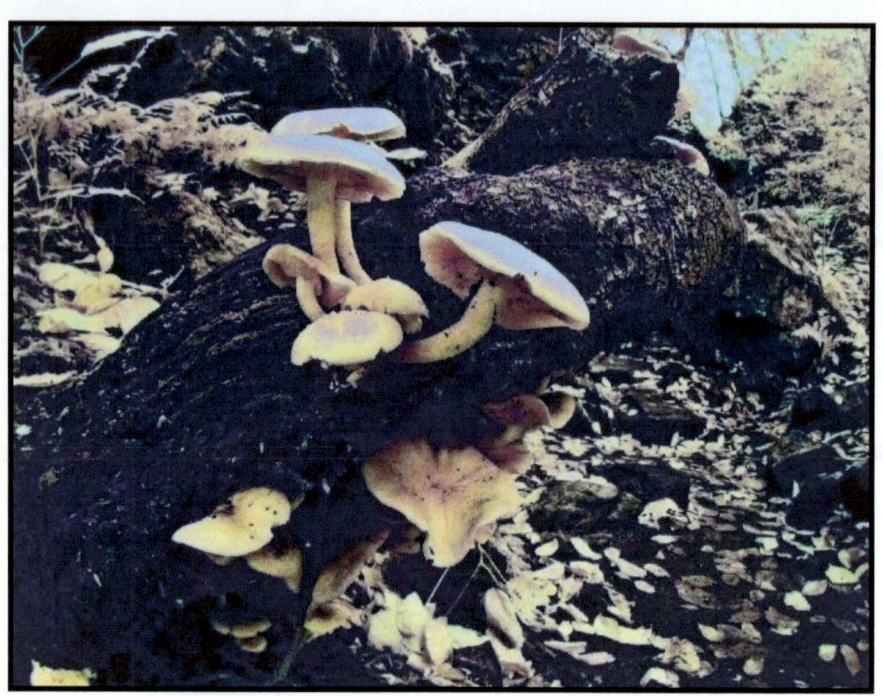

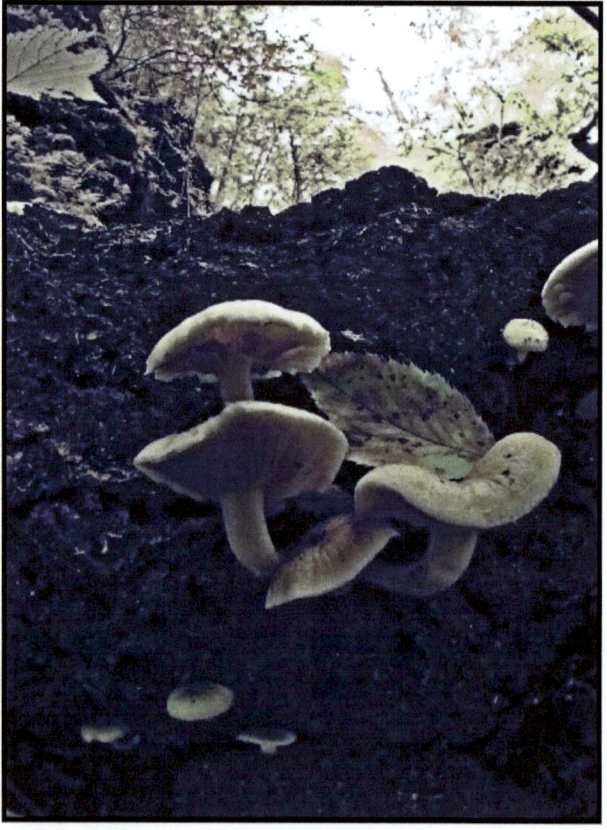

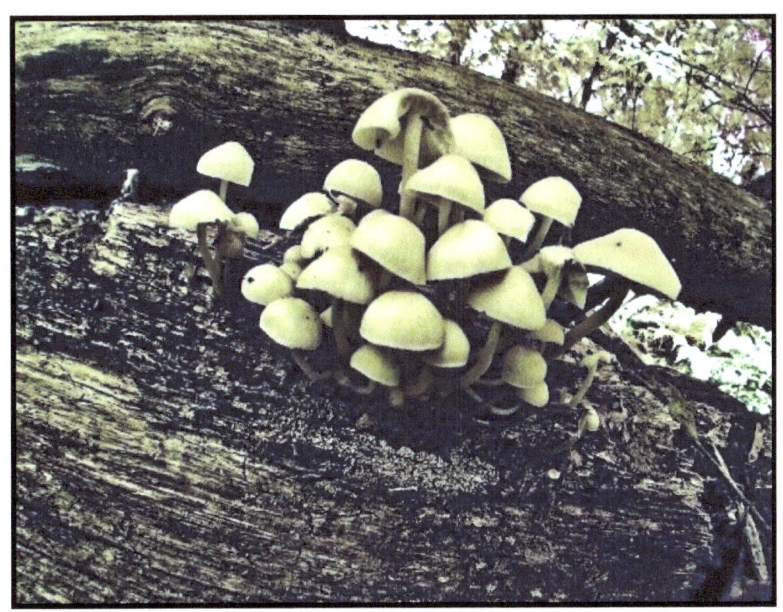

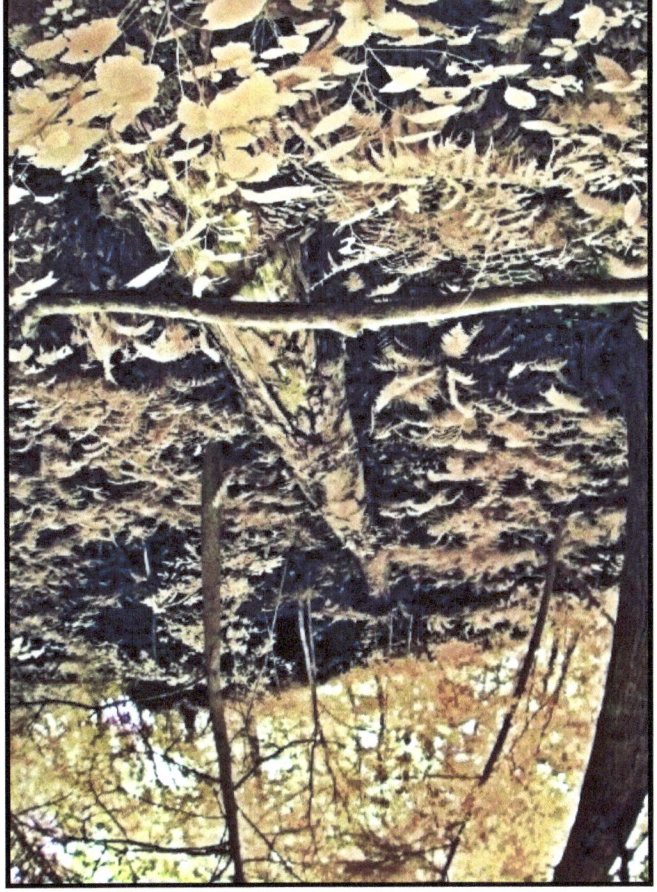

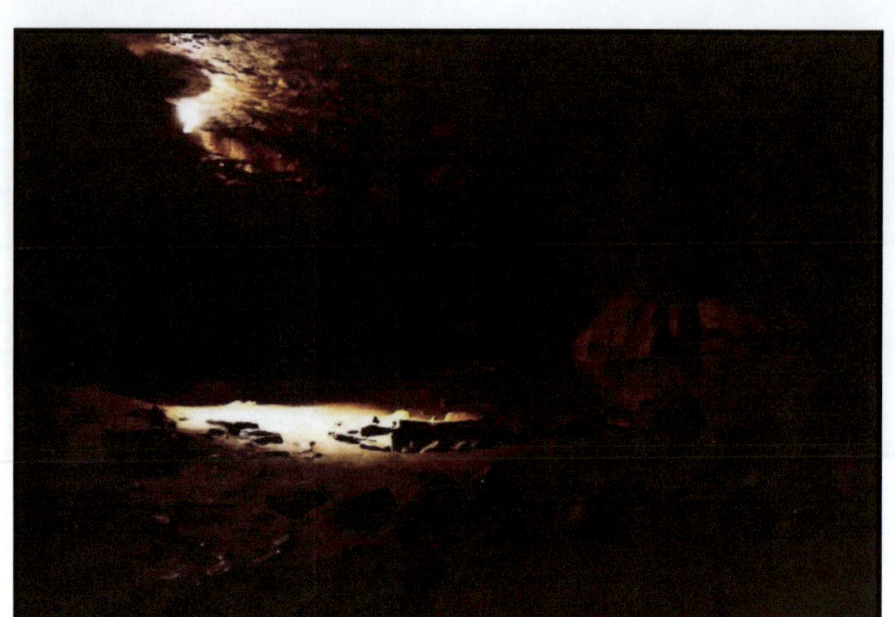

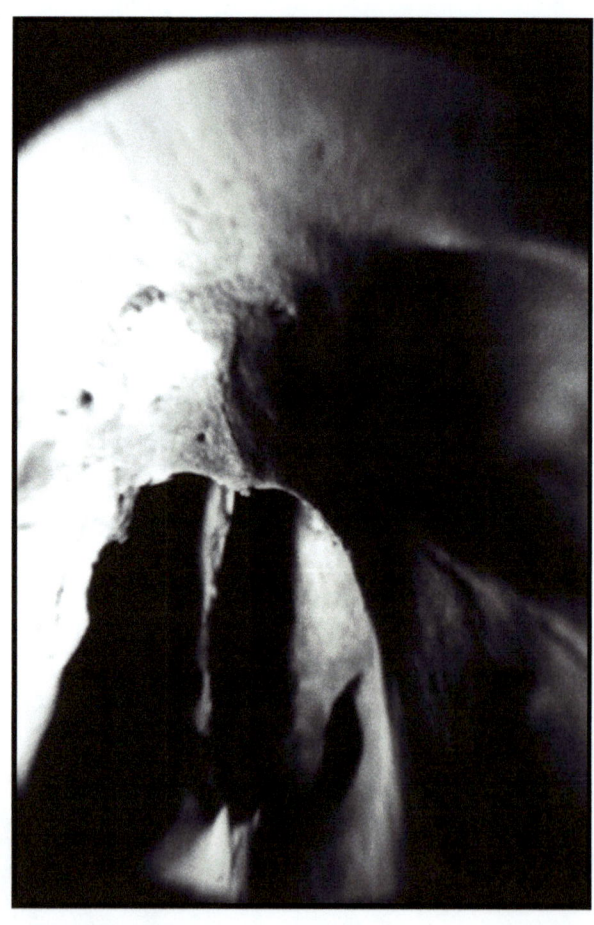

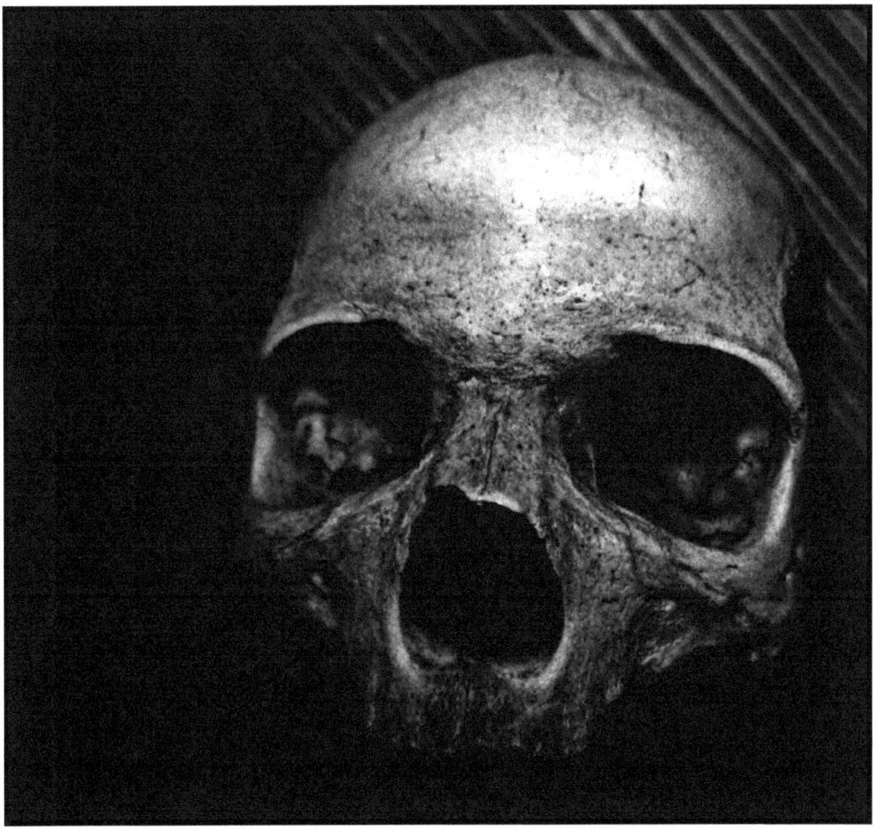

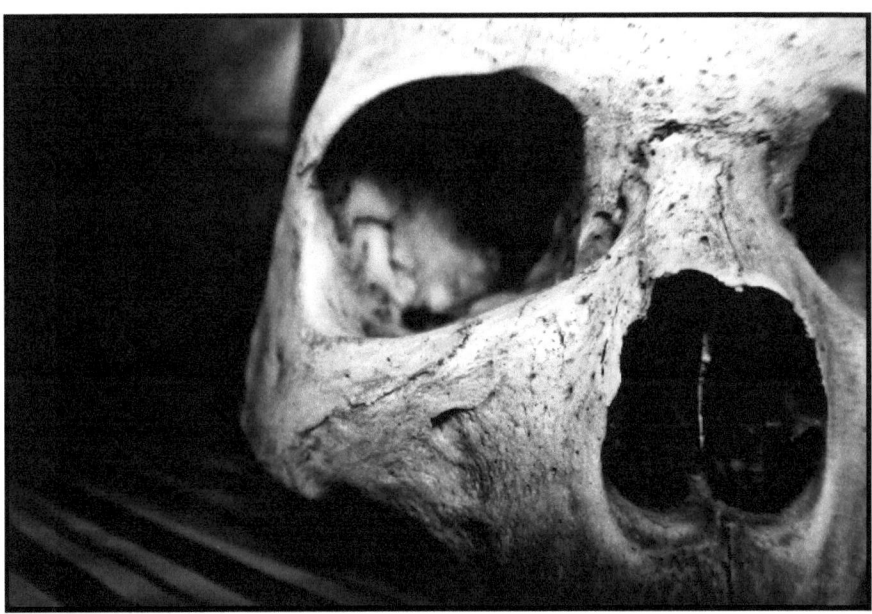

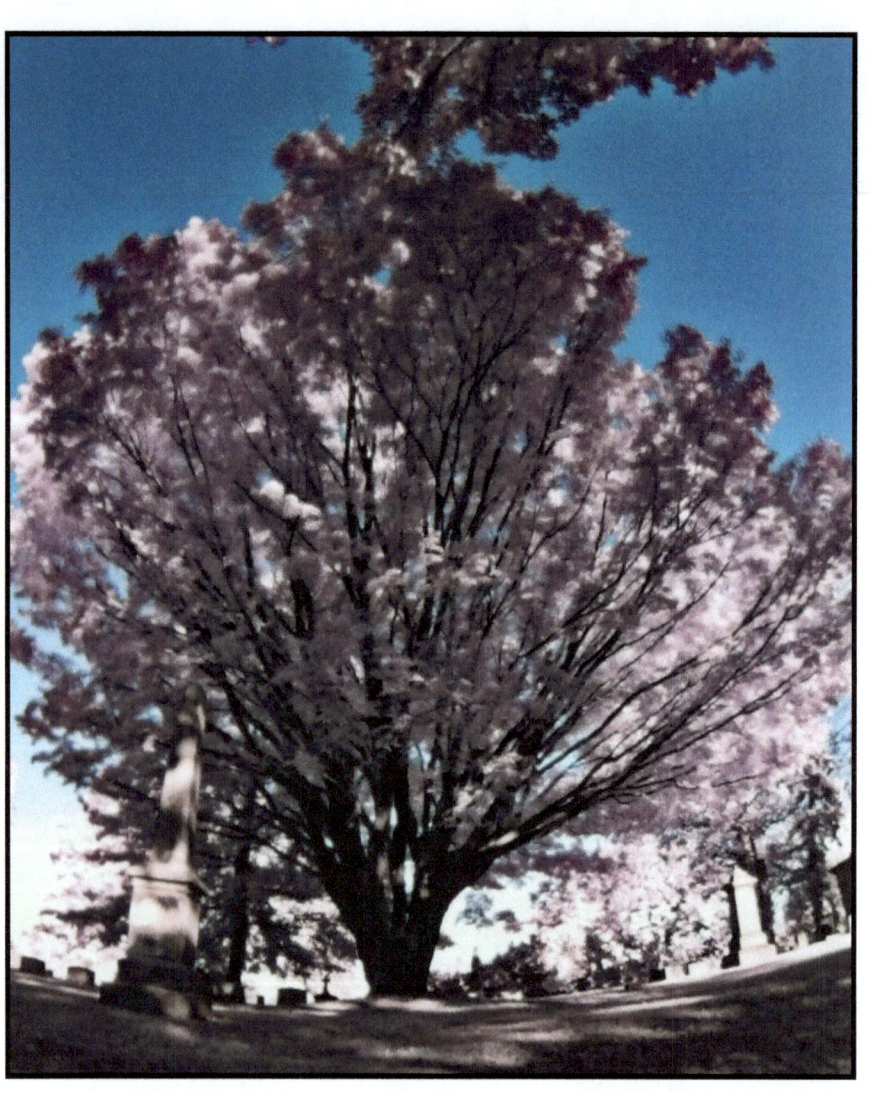

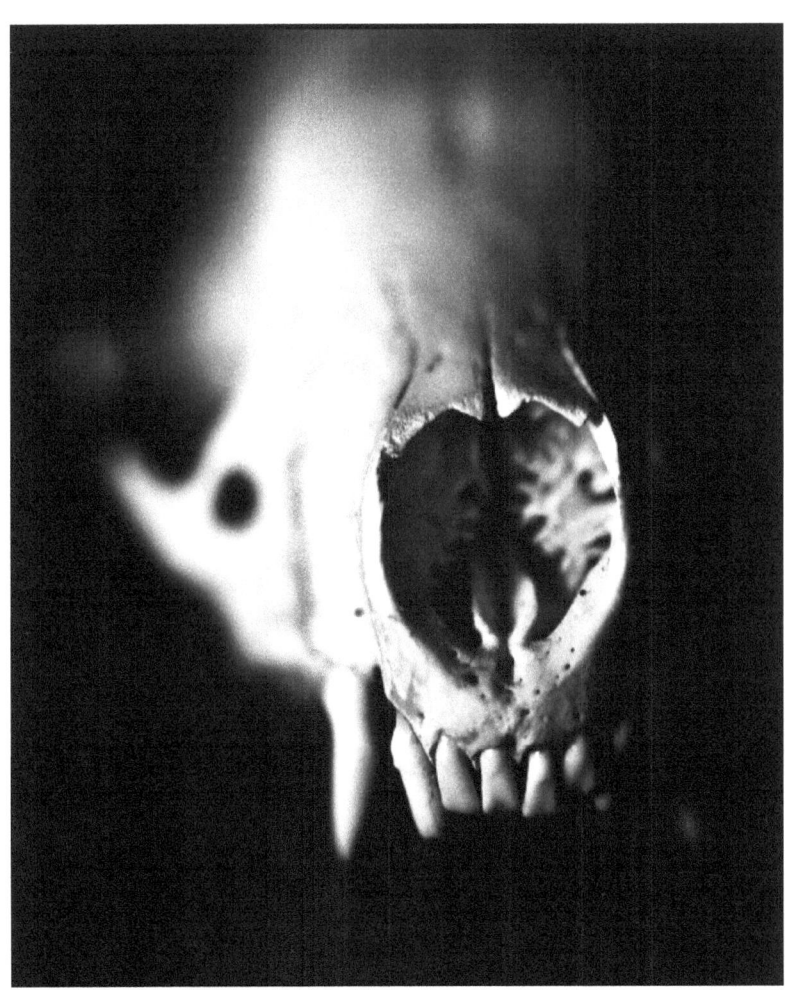

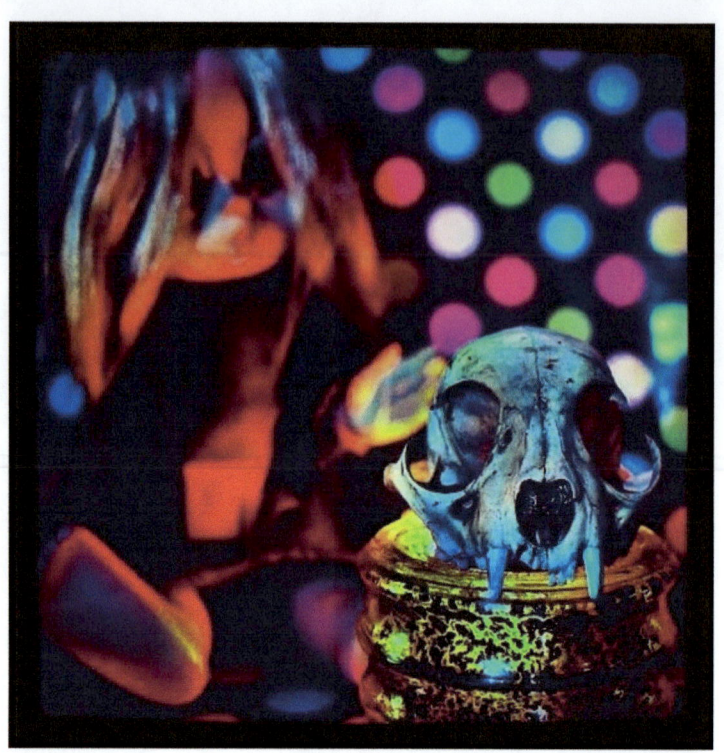

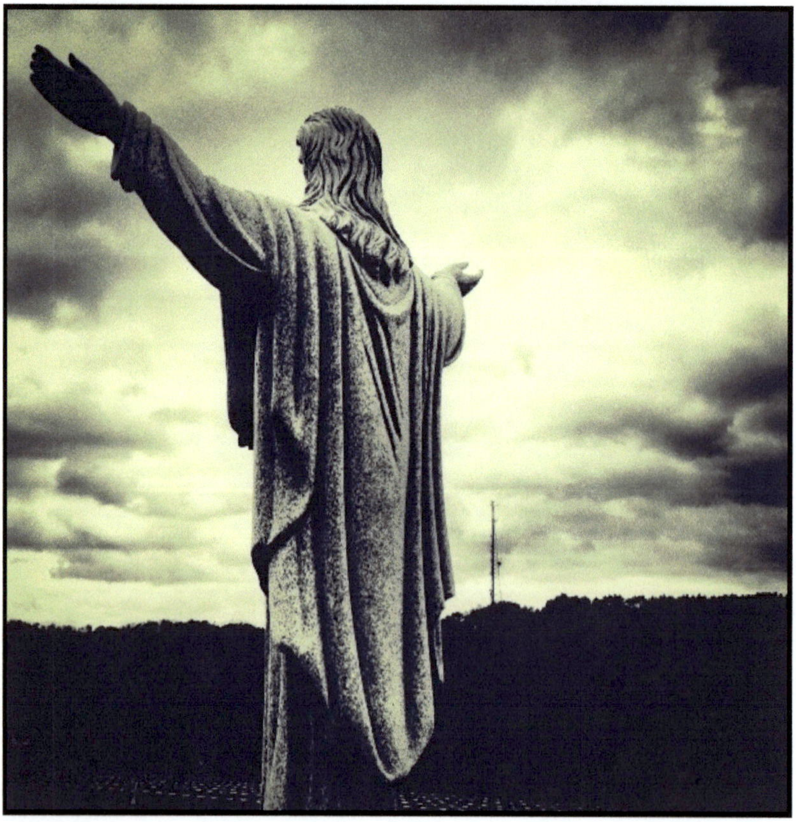

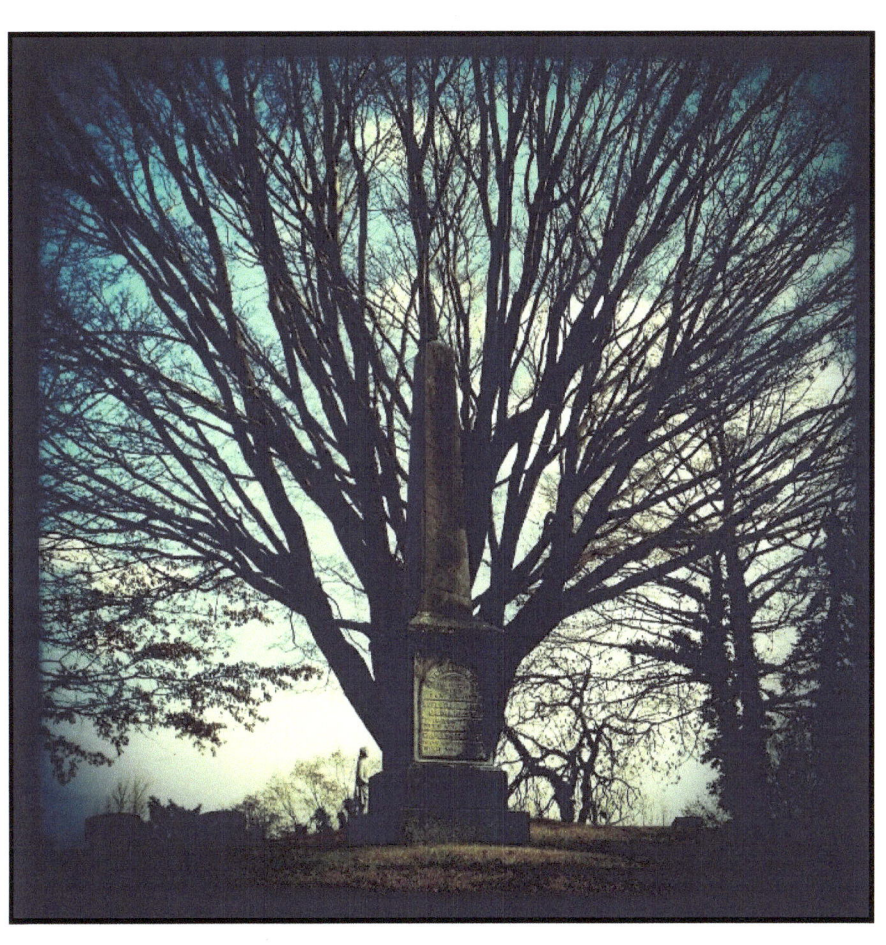

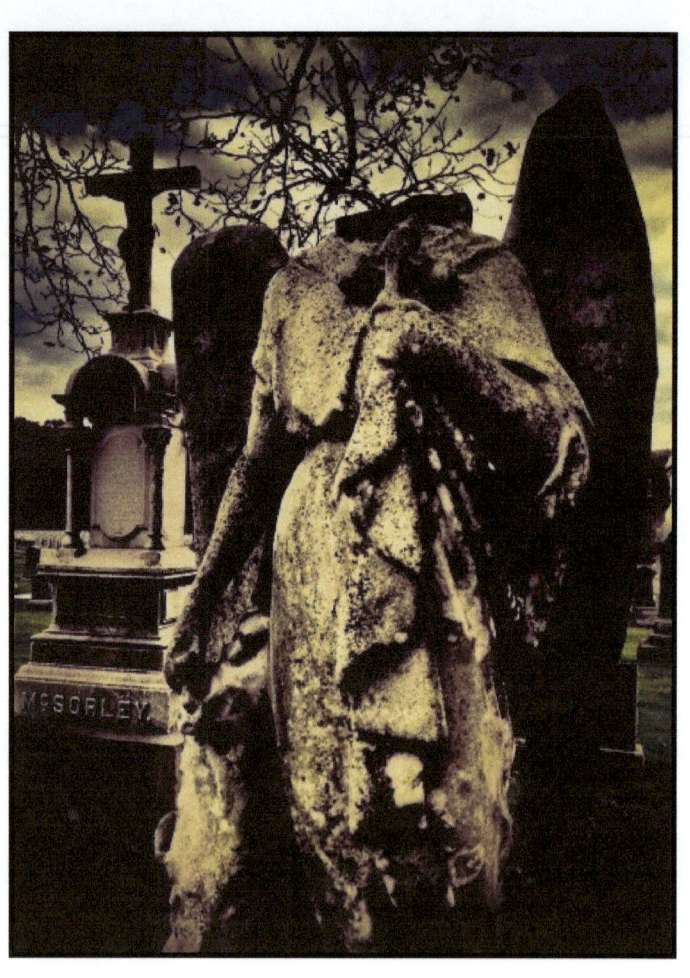

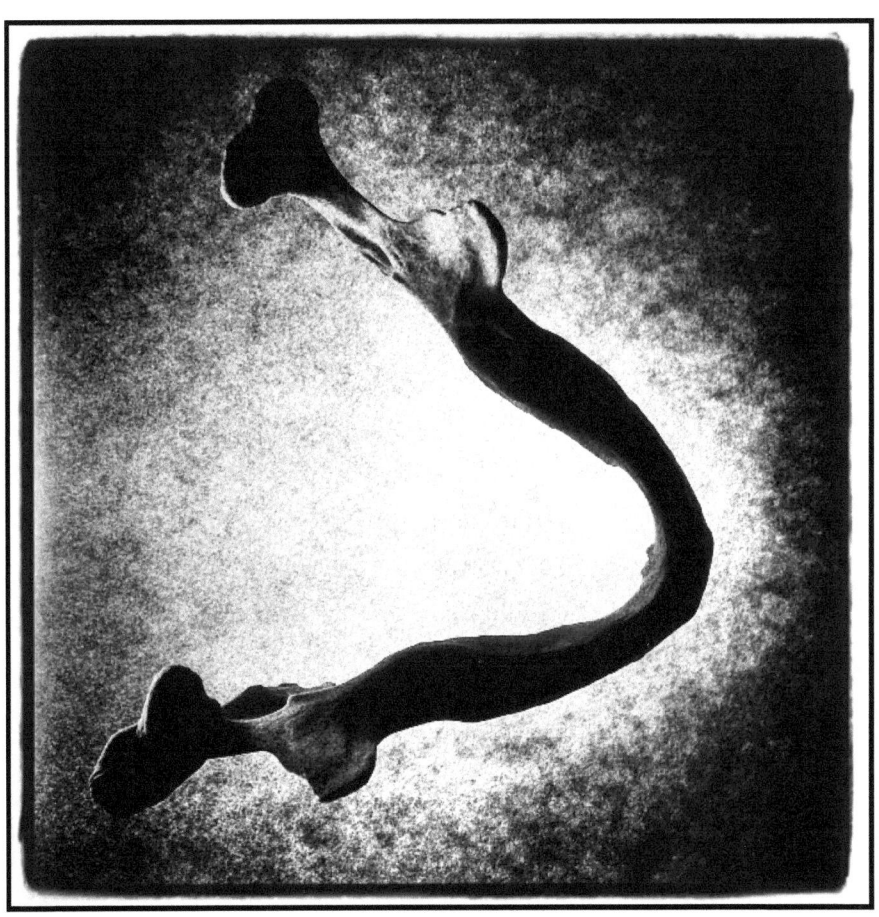

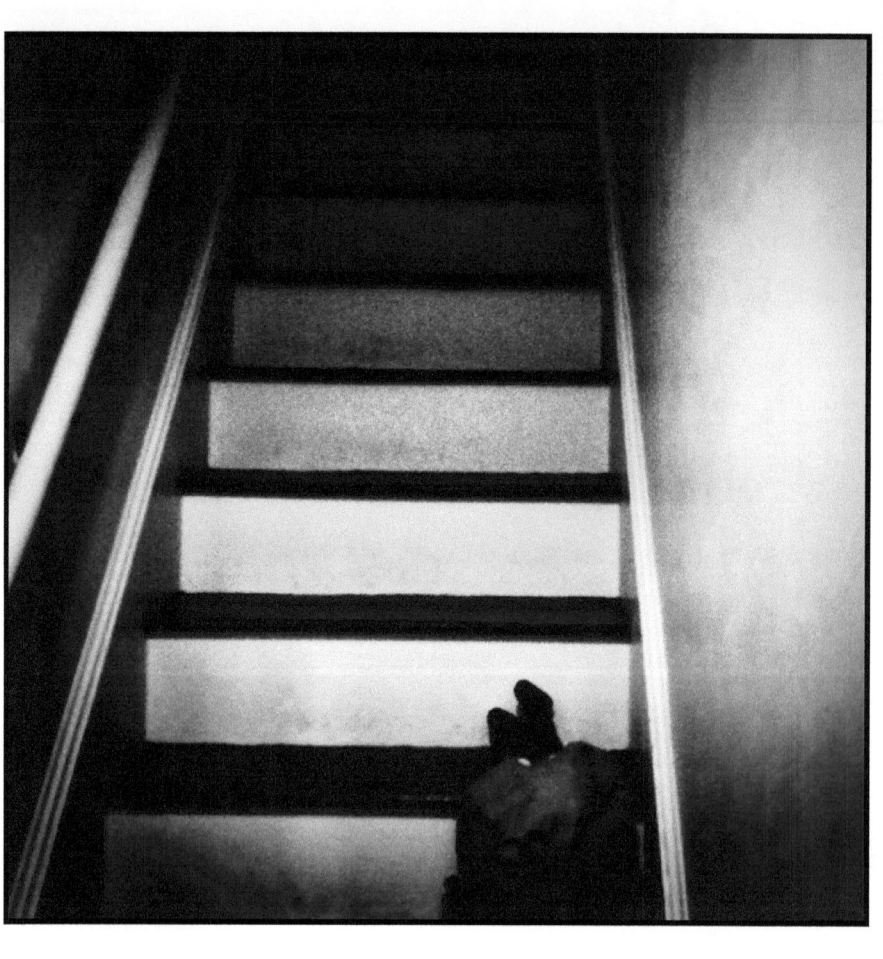

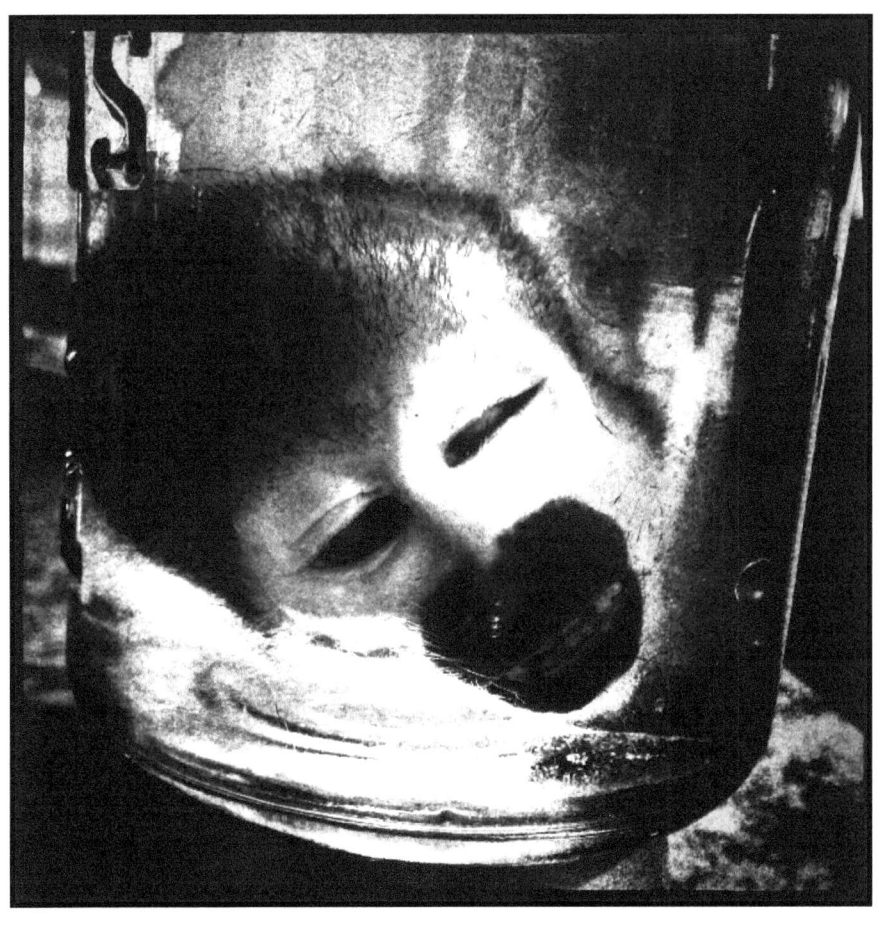

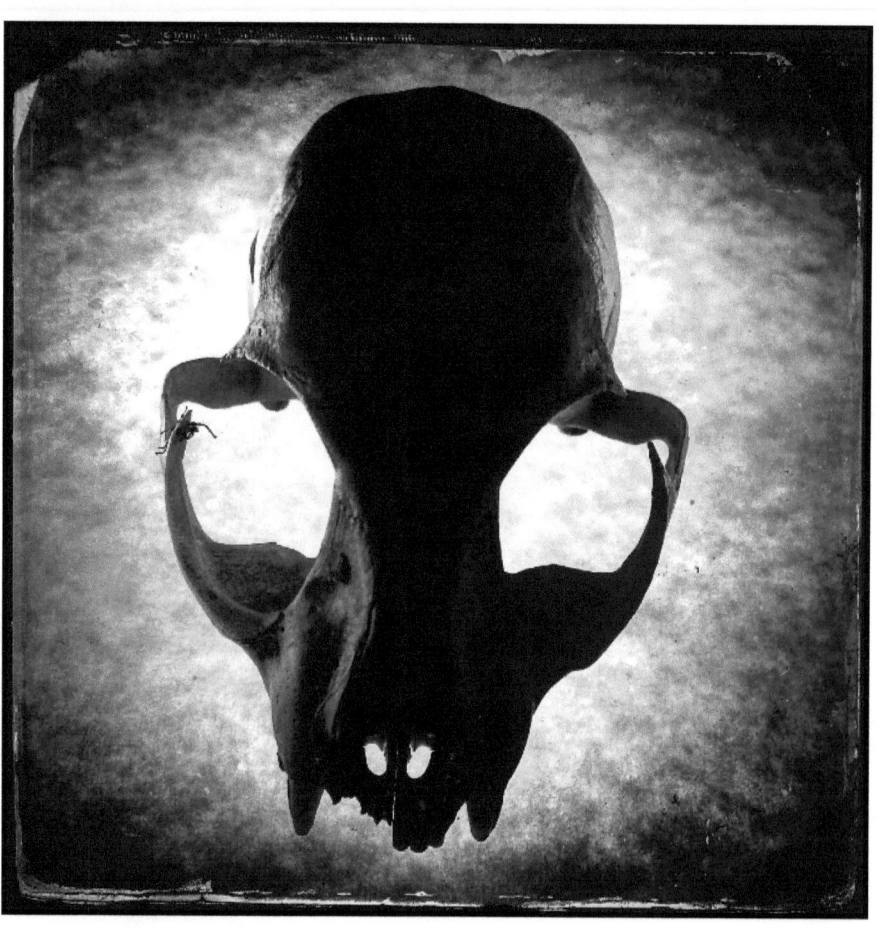

All content by Tom Tooth

FOR MORE

INSTAGRAM:
@TOM_TOOTH
@BOILEDRUGBURNS

RED BUBBLE:
REDBUBBLE.COM/PEOPLE/
BOILEDRUGBURNS

EVERYTHING HERE
IS AND WAS AS
IT WAS MEANT
TO BE.

THE
END.

www.ingramcontent.com/pod-product-compliance
Lightning Source LLC
Chambersburg PA
CBHW040245220526
45473CB00001B/376